TEACHINGS FROM THE ASCENDED MASTERS

BERYL CHARNLEY

Copyright © Beryl Charnley

© Purple Spirit Press 2016

All rights reserved. No part of this publication may be reproduced, stored in a retrieval system, or transmitted in any form or by any means, electronic, mechanical, photocopying, recording or otherwise without the prior permission of the copyright owner.

Original transcription of the channelled work in the 1980's and 1990's by Beryl Charnley
Transcribed and typed by Gordon Charnley
Digital re-formatted to 6" x 9" in 2016 by
Heather Charnley

ISBN 978-1-907042-30-0

PURPLE SPIRIT PRESS
Heather Charnley
Email: purplespiritpress@gmail.com
heathercharnley@googlemail.com
www.heathercharnleyspiritualart.co.uk

**You are welcome to visit the website and see what's new.
Please contact if you wish to have more details.**

Channelled Teachings From the Ascended Masters – Foreword

Teachings by
Jesus (Sananda), and Master Rakoczi (Master R.)

Notes about the Channelled Teachings:

1. The compilation of teachings was begun in 1986 and spanned a duration of about 12 years. They accompanied the family's spiritual unfoldment and so were exciting, reassuring and informative at such a time when there was little information available then.

2. They are a real tool or foundation for those people who are looking for a basis to start out on their own spiritual journeys and need information which speaks clearly and very simply which is useful when there is such a huge array of this information available today to choose from and can cause confusion.

3. The teachings themselves are comprised of the I Am Presence, which is actually from Jesus (now Sananda) and the Master R. (Rakoczi) always the shortened version of his name – he is a European Master whose previous life was as the Comte de Saint Germain.

4. Subjects covered are many – meditation, enlightenment, spirituality, karma and reincarnation, unconditional love, general raising of man's consciousness, attitude to the environment and the transmission of Light to negative areas of the planet where there is violence and negativity.

5. The teachings began very simply from angelic beings who helped to pave the way for me to start channellings at a time when I had never heard of the subject and was rather wary naturally! Sananda asked if I was willing to do the work, which I obviously was honoured to do but unsure of my capabilities. These gave me the confidence to progress to the I Am presence, which followed on from them.

Beryl Charnley

TEACHINGS FROM THE ASCENDED MASTERS

PART ONE

TEACHINGS FROM THE MASTERS
Book One

CONTENTS   Page

Foreword	3
Section 1 – Master Jesus/Sananda	6
Section 2 – Master Jesus/Sananda	10
Section 3 – Master Jesus/Sananda	13
Section 4 – Master Jesus/Sananda	16
Section 5 – Master Jesus/Sananda	19
Section 6 – Master Rakoczi	22
Section 7 – Master Rakoczi	26
Section 8 – Master Rakoczi	29
Section 9 – Master Rakoczi	32
Section 10 – Master Rakoczi	35
Section 11 – Master Rakoczi	38
Section 12 – Master Rakoczi	41
FOR THOSE NEW TO CHANNELLING	45

Channelled by Beryl Charnley

TEACHINGS FROM THE ASCENDED MASTERS-1

Each man and woman living today has chosen to incarnate now to experience all that is happening in the world at present. It is an important incarnation in the fact that there are great happenings abroad – there is turmoil, suffering, and there are changes within the climate. All this was ordained when I was alive. It is difficult to conceive that anyone could ordain this so far ahead, but God has chosen man to live upon the Earth and to choose what he will do within that lifetime. To experience a situation such as you are all experiencing now. Your choice was this situation and although you have experienced other things before you were brought to this situation like others at present, to live through everything that is happening, to do what you are beginning to do now. To work for Me and others like Me.

The Masters of the Hierarchy are sending forth their teachings to many at present upon the Earth. You are one of many, as you know, channelling our words to mankind to allow you to receive wisdom, which has been passed down through the ages, so that you can pass this knowledge that has been arcane on to others. Certain people have known about it, but until it was put into books, this knowledge was secret; part of the Ancient Wisdom, which has been known and used by many. This wisdom has been given to Me and I used much of it during My lifetime, to create miracles from time to time, so that men would take note of what I had to say and do during My life on Earth.

There are many who will not listen until something is proved to them beyond doubt. I know that there are others who have true faith and will believe what is written in the Bible, but parts of the Bible are not truly accurate. Perhaps in their enthusiasm those who wrote it have been carried away with words, or perhaps in the translation there has not been an accurate word for something that has occurred, and so there have been changes within these stories over the years. But I only wish to tell you that all can perform miracles if they will have true faith in what they can do. Humanity is capable of so much more than he anticipates. Through prayer, meditation and faith this can be achieved. The miracles that I performed in this manner and those who do not believe this can think of other people who have achieved so called miracles. Think of those who can walk on hot coals for instance and not be burnt. They could not do this for the length of time it takes them to cross the coals unless they had true faith. This is something that must be thought of.

There are many within the world at present who would be considered to have achieved miracles. There are people who live in high places, literally high places within mountainous regions, who have reached upwards to a very high level of consciousness. I am thinking particularly of those in Tibet, some of whom are lamas, and there are some within other mountainous regions beyond your ken who have also raised their consciousness to a very high level, so that they are aware of the Masters who come and go in this mountainous region of the Himalayas. They can commune with them and they can do the miracles that the Masters achieve, such as levitation and travelling distances which would be unheard of in a short length of time; this is done through positive thought. You can do all things if you will; all things are possible through faith and through prayer. It is not easy to achieve. You must have the will and desire to do this, but mankind is capable of so much more.

For instance, think of an iceberg. It looks absolutely massive when you see it on a film perhaps if you have not experienced seeing it yourself, but think of what is beneath the surface. Usually there is much more below the surface than is showing, it is said that nine tenths of an iceberg is below the surface. Compare that with man and the way he lives, and his mind. Compare how much of his mind he uses during his life and think of how much is hidden beneath the surface and never used. That mind is all-powerful if you can link with God. If you can use your mind to good advantage you can achieve so much that you would never dream of. This mind which man has been given can be used ten times more powerfully than it is at present by most of humanity, and through this, all can perform miracles. If you had the will to do so you could walk on water. If you had the will to do so you could levitate. If you had the will do so you could move yourself from one place to many miles away. All this is possible; think of the fire-walkers and what they have achieved through faith and prayer. They have linked with God; they have reached their consciousness as high as is humanly possible.

All the Masters have achieved this and more. They have mastered everything within a lifetime; within their last lifetime upon Earth. As a result, the Masters of the Hierarchy can come and go out of the spirit world and into the physical world. Those who are spiritually aware have seen them, and sometimes they have been seen by others who did not know who they were. But until you have mastered everything that you wish to achieve in your incarnations, you have not become a Master. The Masters of the Hierarchy have suffered much. They have lived so many times and evolved their spirits to the highest level it is possible to achieve. In this they have become one. You have heard of the White Brotherhood; this is another name for the Masters. The White Brotherhood is a group of beings who have achieved everything within their lifetimes, and they have reached a level of consciousness where they can link permanently with God, and they can visit mankind to help him. They are all one; one with one another; one with humanity if he will accept them, and one with all the High Beings within what you call Heaven.

This is just one plane of the many planes of spiritual being. It is man's home in reality; where he came from and where he returns after each incarnation. So that he can rest awhile after an illness or an accident. Learning whilst he is there and deciding what he will achieve during the time he is in that realm of spirit, and later making a decision regarding his next incarnation before he returns to Earth so that he will have decided where he will live and who his parents will be. As you know, this choice is made and you have free will when you return. As each incarnation goes by, the spirit evolves, and through experience of different situations mankind betters himself, hopefully improving and honing his spirit to a higher level of consciousness and being. There is so much to learn and over the years; over the millennia; mankind is still learning. There are still problems to be solved and suffering to be endured, but if that can help in any way, then it is worthwhile. Karmic rewards are many and sometimes racial Karma can be achieved. This is happening in many parts of the East at present; the peoples of Angola, Somalia and Bosnia are suffering. It is hoped that much will be the reward for these peoples who have chosen to suffer at this time.

In the future; and I do not speak of a long future now, there will be fewer people returning to the Earth, because the Earth is at a point when it will be moving and is doing so now, into a higher dimension. So incarnation will end once this is achieved; that is upon the third dimension. I know that some of you are aware that when you are asleep, you move onto the astral plane, which is the fourth dimension. In dream state you meet up with all sorts of possibilities. You meet other people sometimes, but this is just a part of your normal experience. Gradually, the Earth is moving into the Astral and will eventually be upon the fifth dimension as many other planets are now, with evolved beings upon them. It is possible to be aware and meet others within your dream state, and return on waking, remember what has occurred. This is possible; to move out of the body and be aware of what is happening. Some people have achieved this particularly if they have been at a point where their life is threatened. They have been aware that they were out of the body but this is not necessarily what will be achieved in future times. Your bodies will become less solid, but there are many changes, which will occur in the future.

The Earth itself will change. Its note is already changing to those who are aware of this and the notes of humanity also. Each one of you sounds a note on the etheric as do all living creatures, but the note that you sound is on the spiritual side of your being. You are not aware of this. It is only those in spirit who can hear this and who can see the light of each of humanity. All of you have that light within you and some shine brighter than others. This is part of your being which is important, knowing as you do that each human is spirit then you realise that that spirit is the light within. That divine spark within each one of you, and if you allow this light to shine forth, knowing of your spirituality, the higher your awareness, the brighter the light. So it is up to each one of you to burnish that light within; to make it shine forth stronger as your life goes by. Reaching upwards so that your consciousness is as high as you can be, so you are aware of God.

There are many things that can be achieved in a lifetime through faith and through the use of the mind. It is all-powerful. When you have achieved a link with God; that powerful link which you will be aware of once you have become dedicated, then you will know that you can achieve much more than you have ever previously done in your life through the mind. Then you will be becoming aware of the Ancient Wisdom, and We can give you all wisdom if you link with the Masters of the Hierarchy. I think that I have covered as much as I wish to today, and I hope that this first teaching will make your minds turn around and make you realise what is possible within your life. God bless and keep you. Master Jesus/Sananda.

TEACHINGS FROM THE ASCENDED MASTERS-2

Upon the world today there are many searchers after truth; it has been so since the world began, and if you can look into your hearts you will realise that you are searching for the truth. That truth is within each one of you if you will listen and raise your thoughts into the realms above; you will hear that still small voice who will teach you the truth; the Ancient Wisdom that men have been seeking over the millennia. I come to you to attempt to give you this truth. I myself was a seeker and during my lifetimes on Earth and elsewhere I have found that the only way to gain this wisdom is to set aside some time each day to meditate and to be quiet within. I know that in your busy lives it is difficult to always find time for this, but unless this is done regularly, you will find that you can soon forget, forget to set aside that time for peace and stillness and always be busy. Just try to BE for a while each day and then you will find that peace within, which you cannot find in the outside world.

So many people have absorbing active lives and it is difficult to fit something, which is nebulous into that life. They feel that the inner life is not the reality. They feel that they have not time to spare to just be. I know that particularly those with young children are consumed all day by activity and noise, but there is always a little time, even quarter of an hour that can be set aside to just be and listen. Truth will be revealed in time. It all takes time to get used to listening for that inner voice, but that truth will be revealed eventually. I know that there are many books around now, which deal with Ancient Wisdom. Many things have been revealed over the recent decades that would not have been considered some time ago. It would have been thought to be witchcraft in centuries past, but now the truth is being revealed to many who are presently living upon the Earth, and fortunately they have written about what they have been given, so that others may learn and this is good, because we hope that this truth will be passed on to all who will listen to you. Sometimes I know it falls on stony ground, but never fear, there is always someone who is wishing to learn new truths. Some people have a barrier around them; their minds are closed to the realities of life. They perhaps think that what they know is best, and maybe it is for them; they are not ready to receive that truth which you can hear when the time is right; when you are ready to hear the truth, it will be revealed.

In my incarnation in Palestine, I had a very interesting life; a life that brought together many people; many throngs of people from time to time who wished to learn, and I was able to teach in different ways, both through the spoken word and through action. In the spoken word I was given much that I passed on to others. Sometimes I was led completely by the Father who spoke through me to the multitudes from time to time. All the words that I was given were inspired. The parables I spoke were given to me directly from above. At other times I was given the gift of healing and was able to perform miracles of healing through the Christ Light from God. I was an instrument in bringing through the spoken word, the healing touch and other miracles that occurred, which demonstrated how the truth from God can be given in different ways. Other miracles that occurred were just to convince people who were doubtful about the capabilities I had, so that in performing these miracles, those who were doubtful were convinced that what I was preaching was genuine. When I turned the water into wine was another instance, when it was difficult for people to provide the wine. At a time when food and sustenance were needed, I performed the miracle of the loaves and fishes for the multitude who became hungry as time went by, and who were utterly convinced when this occurred. It was not for my own benefit or for my power or glory; it was purely for the glory of God and for the benefit of those who were around me.

I know that most people who wish to know the Ancient Wisdom do not want power; they just wish to know the truth about life and its purpose and what to aim for within that lifetime. Those who wish for power are not interested in the Ancient Wisdom as such, unless it is something that will benefit them, and so I speak to the man in the street. Those whom I spoke to when I last incarnated; the simple people who only wish to know what they must do in their lives. Others who wish for more complicated truth, who are perhaps more academic, will be able to read this in more detail in other books which are available; for instance, Alice Bailey's books, which contain a great deal of detail, and are excellent. Most people who are searching for truth will find that what I have to say is more direct. I do not wish to assume that everyone who listens to me is not intelligent, but only that they prefer my direct way of putting things, rather than a style which is more complex.

When you look around, you see how people seem to be attracted to violent programmes on television and the same with books. It is strange how peoples' minds seem to turn to violence. I think that the media are just creating this for the masses because they crave excitement, but they are not content with normal adventure stories in books or on films. They have to have something that is more extreme and attractive to their evil side. Each person has two sides to their nature, although most wish that they had not. People have this sadistic streak and perhaps those who seek for truth and try to be harmless in their lives push aside this side of their nature, but those who look for violence in their entertainment are allowing the evil side of their nature to come to the surface and at this present time upon the world evil often seems to be taking over, and where there is genuine suffering, particularly in those countries e.g. Bosnia where there has been violence and fighting for so long.

Have faith; good will overcome this evil that has been rampaging for some time. I know at present you feel that it is impossible this will occur, but have faith and try to project positive thoughts towards those countries where battles still rage. You can help if you will, by projecting positivity and light, because this will help to bring an end to the violence and help the innocent people who are involved, by sending forth light and healing towards these areas. Many of you do this I know, but I encourage anyone else who has not already done so to join in this work of the World Servers. There has been much good done over the years by those who are aware of this truth, that healing light and love can all be sent from their minds to others in need and over the years this has served those people in need and benefited them greatly.

It was through the Great Invocation given to Alice Bailey from the Master D.K. that these thoughts began and the Group of World Servers became well known over the years, and has spread and done so much for suffering humanity. This truth is part of what has been searched for by many and it can be spread to more as time goes by. Always keep this in mind, that truth can be given to all; all who wish to help and to do good in the world, and I am hoping that in time to come, more and more will link in this way to spread healing and love, so that the plan will come to pass; God's plan for humanity; the linking of minds to do good. At present the evil that is around has been spreading, but the negative side, the evil side of man's nature must be overcome by good and by love.

Love can conquer all. Love is all-powerful and can create a wonderful power for good, and if it is projected from the heart powerfully and positively, then anything can be overcome. Believe and it will come to pass; you can do all things through Christ. That is how I overcame evil in the world through sending forth my love to all men and giving of myself for that purpose, so that all can receive love and give forth love, and man continues in his lifetimes to learn this truth. I know that all are searching so that they can evolve and improve their capabilities as each lifetime goes by. Be assured that the truth will be given unto you and I will do all in my power to give forth of this truth in many teachings as time goes by. God bless and keep you. Master Jesus/Sananda.

TEACHINGS FROM THE ASCENDED MASTERS-3

I am the Light of the World; you are My Light in the world. Remember this in whatever you do in your lives. Try to be true examples of the light. You are children of the light and I say unto you spread that light to all men; the word of God that I give to you. God created the world and all that therein is. He created man in His image to do His work for Him in the world, and I trust that you and all men will spread My word. If you behold someone who is in trouble you try to help them and whenever there is trouble about it brings out the best in all people. It is at times such as war against another country, that you treat your fellow men as brothers, but this is not always so and we hope that in time to come, humanity will realise what his task is; just to be a brotherhood; a brotherhood of men throughout the world, attempting to live as brothers with no wars, no violence or crime; to just be as we had hoped that you would be. I know that it is difficult to always be as you should and I know that temptations come, and at times you feel that you wish to be, as you yourself want.

It is difficult not to be selfish at times, but attempt to think of others before yourselves, and attempt to reach up your consciousness to a higher level; always striving to reach to the realms above when you sit quietly in your meditation time. This is a time of quiet; the time when your spirituality becomes the most important part of you that has existed over the many lifetimes in which you have participated. The higher self is the part that knows all, and it is that part of you which you make whole in your meditation, linking your lower self with your higher self, so that you become one and this is what we are attempting to teach; the oneness of life, so that in linking with the higher realms, you become one with the Universal Mind.

When you pass into spirit, when that transition takes place at the end of this lifetime that is what happens; you become one with the Universal Mind; the Cosmic Consciousness. It has many names, but it is the link, which you have when you are upon the Earth; this is the link with the spiritual realms. Your higher self lives upon this realm and you return home to this realm at the time of your transition into spirit. Therefore, it is most important to keep this link, to not be too separate in your life; so many people wander lost and alone, not knowing that they truly belong to this oneness. Those who have not discovered their spirituality; those sad people who try to find help in other ways, but if they would just realise that within them there is all knowledge. Within them is the power to link with God, because each one of you has that spark of divinity within you, and this knowledge helps all who are aware of the oneness of mankind with the Cosmic Consciousness; this is what makes life worthwhile. The evolution of the soul is what is required of man through his lifetimes; honing his spirit to a higher level as each incarnation goes by, so that he can reach up in each lifetime to a higher vibratory level than before. This linking with light keeps that spark shining forth within you; that divine spark which is all-important.

In choosing to live now, humanity is learning many things. It is a time of transition within the world. With the violence that is existent in many parts of the world, it is a learning time to break through to better times. There is always darkness before the dawn as they say, and it is through this darkness that the Phoenix will rise from the ashes, and new life; new meaning of life will begin, but it is important to know that you should send forth positive thought and light towards all these places where so much help is required. Positivity and light will break through the darkness and evil and bring good, and spread peace throughout the world at this time of trouble. There have always been wars and rumours of wars, but in this age of Kali, it is a time where there is much turmoil and much help required from all of you. Whether you are involved in this war or not, you can involve yourselves by helping to send forth love and light because love means light, and this is what is required in the world at this time. Unconditional love for all.

This is something that is quite difficult because mankind always judges; he judges by appearances and appearances can be deceptive. It is very easy to scoff at those who are different, perhaps by colour of skin or way of living, but try not to judge lest you yourselves by judged. God should be the only one to judge at any time, remember this. When I lived upon the Earth, I too was judged and found wanting by those who were in charge, even though I was trying to spread the word of God to all. There were some who twisted My words and this is what each one of you must guard against. The words that are twisted can be those that condemn you and others, so remember how it was for Me and how, although I knew what My end would be, it came very swiftly. I had within My group one who betrayed Me, and caused Me to be humiliated and taken away from My work; from God's work; but this was part of My destiny and I gave My life for others that all men should know that they could rise again and be immortal as I am.

I speak to many at this time; over two thousand years after My birth, and I know that sometimes it is doubted that I speak, but truly I am the Light of the World, and My presence is most important at this time; to try to guide mankind in ways of peace. There are many Masters of the Hierarchy who speak to mankind at this time through those who channel our words. We only hope that we can give hope to mankind for future days, because there is much to look forward to in the future. Mankind can break through this morass of violence and bring hope and joy to all. The way to this new life is through prayer and meditation. I know that most of you who read this already do so, but meditation is an important part of praise to God. The Eastern religions have always taught this, but it is in the West that it must be made known. The importance of this daily routine to set aside a time each day to be yourselves, to cast aside all doubts, all troubles and just listen for that small voice within. Many times I would go into the wilderness to be on My own and to commune with the realms above; with God. I had to get away from people from time to time, and it was only in this way that I could be quiet. Each one of you needs this time to be alone; to commune; it is important. It is good to meet people in your daily round, but there is still that short time when you should have your own space around you, so that you can be one with God.

People talk of separation, the separation from the spirit; that part of you, the higher self which is always living in the spirit world, and which you link with in meditation, and therefore you must try to keep this oneness within you so that you never feel alone or apart. No one need be alone; they can always know that there is someone who will help them in time of trouble if they have that link with the Divine. So many people have lost this capability of linking with the realms above, and it is important that they should relearn this so that they can be a part of the whole reality; the reality of the world of light. Your life on Earth is precious and should be used to the full; all life is precious. Never harm anything, which is living because it is part of God. Remember this when you see something that you do not like; perhaps an insect or an animal, and shudder at the sight of it, but it is part of God's creation and everything within creation is precious to God. Try to remember this in your daily life, and then nothing need be killed until the time when it dies naturally and passes into dust and becomes part of everything once more.

We wish to spread the word to all men and we hope that in time, there will be an understanding that was lost and is found. God bless, Master Jesus/Sananda.

TEACHINGS FROM THE ASCENDED MASTERS-4

At this time of peace and goodwill We think of the Christmas story and We hope that the peace and goodwill present now will continue throughout the years to come, so that love will conquer evil and violence. On thinking about the Christmas story, there are many who have this uppermost in their hearts at this time of year; spreading this word to all and sending out love to those with whom they are in touch. The presents that they send represent the presents that were given to the baby Jesus at the time of His birth by the wise men who came from afar. It was the star that led them; the Christ Star over Bethlehem. The wise men represent those who have an awareness of their spirituality, this spiritual awareness has been increasing throughout the world over the past few decades; a raising of consciousness and more awareness of the 'raison d'être' of life, and I know that those who are reading these words are aware, but many in those days were not.

At that time when that star shone in the sky, there were many who were frightened, and they felt that it was a threat to them of some kind. They did not know what it was, so they sought shelter and ran indoors hoping that it would go away. There were others who had a sense of wonder in their hearts; those simple shepherds, some of who were a little frightened but in their simplicity they accepted this star and felt that perhaps it was something wonderful to worship. There were others who sensed that this star meant a threat to their entitlement, rather like Herod, who felt that he was under threat of losing his kingdom, having heard that a king was to be born, and he could not understand this. He did not realise that it was not the kingdom of the Earth but the kingdom of Heaven that was represented by the Christ child.

Those wise men who followed the star came with their gifts that represented an inner meaning. One brought gold and laid it by the manger, one brought frankincense and the other one brought myrrh. The gold represented the truth that is in the hearts of all men who are pure, and it represents that thread of gold that runs through each lifetime, becoming more powerful as another facet of the whole is learnt. As each incarnation goes by, a little more gold shines forth to others. The frankincense represented the spirituality of man as it does when incense is burnt in many temples of worship throughout the world. The smoke, which is spiralling into the air, represents a prayer; a reaching up to the higher realms by that individual who is burning the incense, who is raising his consciousness to a higher level, and the incense sharpens the senses. The myrrh that was given, was given in loyalty; a precious substance from the east that is only given to those of royal birth. Therefore, those three gifts were very apt; given by those who were aware of the meaning of that birth.

Jesus was born in a stable. He was laid in a manger and He had a simple life. I was that baby born to Mary and Joseph; simple people who lived in a small town, and I was brought up as other children were in those days. I led a simple life always and tried to speak to all who would accept My words; the words of God, in as direct a way as possible, and this is how We hope that you will be; as a child accepting My words and passing them on to all who will listen. The Christmas story is in the minds of many today; those who have time to think about it at this time of year, but so many are rushing about with their families in an active life. It is only on Christmas Day that they will dwell on the Christmas story, and perhaps give thought to that when they sing carols and bend the knee in Church, so that they commune with others throughout the world.

In these many years since I was born; almost two thousand years ago, the word has spread across the world to those of the Christian faith, and although all that time has gone by, each year celebrating the Christ Mass brings out the best of humanity. That star which rose in the east was sent for a purpose guiding those in the past and guiding mankind now and in the future. If that star was seen nowadays with the knowledge of astronomy, which was not available in those days, many would think that it was a new planet or perhaps a super nova, or there are some still who might feel threatened as they were in the past, and run indoors hoping that it will go away. Others might look at it and think that it might be a spaceship with a sense of excitement, and feel that perhaps something will be happening shortly. It is as well to have an open mind and a mind that will accept new thoughts; apart from those which were given so long ago with the Christmas story; new thoughts about those who dwell on distant planets, because it is perfectly possible that it could be a space craft.

I only wish to pass on this thought, that if men will keep their minds open and spread goodwill and peace to all; at all times throughout the year; not just at Christmas, so that goodness and love will prevail and overcome the evil and violence that is present in the world. Try to think of those places where this is occurring and send out positive love and light to these areas, so that the goodness and light will overcome the evil, as it always does in time. It is just that at this time it is prevalent, but I know that much is being done to help these suffering people throughout the world. The Christmas story is spreading, and many towns and countries are helping at this Christmas time to send love and presents to those unfortunate children who have suffered much. I know that in your hearts you wish to send forth love to them yourselves.

Throughout the time that I dwelt in My country, I tried to give forth love; unconditional love to all, even when I walked to Calvary with the cross, I loved and forgave those who had betrayed and humiliated Me towards the end of My lifetime, but as you know, that was not the end of My existence, and throughout that time since the Crucifixion I have dwelt in men's' hearts as I have dwelt in the realms above. I have been sending forth My love and words to those upon the Earth over the years, through communications such as these, so that all might know My thoughts, and spread My words to others, that they may know the truth. Then that gold of truth will shine forth to all that they too will accept and spread this truth, and spread the spirituality represented by the frankincense to all, giving forth precious gifts such as I received so that all will receive these gifts of love and peace. I send forth My love and peace to the world at this time, and give My blessing to all. God bless, Master Jesus/Sananda.

TEACHINGS FROM THE ASCENDED MASTERS-5

The future is bright for all of true faith. There is much talk of gloom and doom and catastrophe to come, but for those who have faith in the Lord, there is nothing to fear. All will be well and the day will dawn when brightness, goodness and truth will be the norm. Those who have the faith to withstand this darkness that prevails will be guided. You know that you have within you that divinity; that true divine spark from God. That is the part of you that has lived forever, and if you can link with that inner reality, you will be aware that all men are spiritual beings and as such, they should be a brotherhood within the world. At present it is most disjointed; broken up, and needing to be unified through faith. It is true that at present there is much that is evil and violent in parts of this Earth, but I am aware that most of you who believe, know that good will prevail, and that the violence which keeps breaking out in certain areas will be overcome.

I have said before that if you will send out light to these places, then it will overtake the darkness, and you will find that in time to come, there will be less danger of violence and you will also find that the people there have become strong in faith, and will manage to overcome the ravages of war, and set their countries to rights with the benefit of your prayer, and with the light that you have sent forth from your hearts. It is strange that many are unaware of this capability of sending forth light from within; they have never discovered their capabilities in this way. It is hoped that in future times, all men will find this which is latent within them, and be able to send forth love, light and healing to others which many of you are presently doing, but there is still a large percentage of people who are capable of this and are unaware of it.

It is a gift from God that all men can use. It was something that I was aware of from an early age. I knew that if I searched within Me I could find an inner strength and a capability that I Myself could never have had without God's help. I knew that I was capable of giving healing to those who came to Me; those who had the knowledge and the faith that I was able to heal them. They knew not how, but they knew that there was within Me this power. The healing power was only a part of the capability that I had given to Me from God. As you know, I did many things which appeared to be miracles, but all this was God given and something which I knew that if I could bring out that power from within, I could do whatever I decided was necessary at the time. I searched within for this and brought it forth. Many things can be done through faith, and if you have that powerful faith, you too can perform miracles. As I have said, the healing light can be sent forth from God, and given by you to others; if you have the faith that God is working through you, all of you can use this capability.

I know that at times when you try to send forth healing, you feel that you have perhaps done nothing to help, but something has been given even if it is not the healing that was hoped for. On a different level, something has been given to that patient. He has been uplifted or renewed in some way, and perhaps the next time something more will be given. It is not always God's will that someone will receive a complete healing at any time. When I performed miracles of healing, it was God's will that those who were crippled should walk, and those who were blind should see, so that all should know His power through Me, because at that time it was necessary to prove to all men that this was possible through My power from God, that all men should believe and have faith in God. It was His will that I should be His instrument and to show that it could be so. Through My power as the Christ, I was given this extremely powerful capability in order to give men faith at that time, but other men can do this work also in a lesser way to begin with. God needed to create a more dramatic gesture at the time when I was alive, so that I could do all things for all men, and perform miracles during the time that I was a Christed One, so that for those three years many miracles were performed in His name.

Time will come when miracles will be performed quite regularly and you will know what it is to be acting in God's name. I know that you feel at present that this could not be, so even though you wish it to be so at times, but times are changing, and your capabilities and bodies are subtly changing even now. As you know, the third dimension that you are on at present will no longer be so in future times; you will be living on a higher dimension. As time goes by, the Earth and those upon it are changing gradually; at times it will be quite dramatic, but you will find that you will be able to cope and that the changes upon the Earth will be overcome. At present there are many changes occurring. Fires are breaking out and causing great hazard and disruption in certain areas, and in other areas rains have come and flooding is occurring. All these things have happened from time to time, but they are becoming more frequent. Great gales have occurred, tornadoes, and there has been damage in other areas of this kind; as I say, they have happened before, but they are becoming more frequent.

Mankind will learn to live with this and manage to overcome it, but all these things are a part of the change which is occurring upon the Earth, and although beautiful forests have been cut down and altered, the climate throughout the world in the past, and at present also, this has nothing to do with the changes that are happening at present. You will find that things will settle down in time, but people should be warned that more flooding can occur and more disruption to the Earth. Just be prepared to protect your property and yourselves. You will find that you will be given protection and warning if anything is likely to occur which will be hazardous in your area. I know that you have faith, and this will bring you through everything that will occur over the next decade. Have faith in Us and We will guide you through this transition and bring you through to a bright new beginning. As I have said at the beginning of this teaching, there is much to look forward to, and you will find that life has much more meaning than it has had recently.

The young people of today have much more to look forward to than they have at present, and their purpose in life will have more meaning. Be assured that all will be well, and that life will be simpler, happier and less violent. Be assured that that new beginning will bring forth great things. Mankind will be capable of wonderful things that you could not imagine at present. Just have faith and know that it will be so, and guidance will be given to all. Listen within you for that still small voice whenever you feel the need for guidance and upliftment, and all will be revealed unto you in due course. God bless and keep you all. Master Jesus/Sananda.

TEACHINGS FROM THE ASCENDED MASTERS-6

There is within the core of each man and woman born upon the Earth a tiny seed of truth. This seed can be nurtured and will be so if that man or woman has the mind to learn truth as time goes by; the seed will then flourish and blossom as the learning continues. There are times when this knowledge can be given to all if they will listen within to the truth that is there within them. It can be immediate; this is being given at present through the consciousness of one who channels My words. It has to be learnt, this capability of reaching within or learning to raise the consciousness to a higher level than the mundane. If each man continues always on the mundane level; never learning to reach within; that little seed of truth can lie dormant forever, never opening upwards and reaching towards its capability. It is strange that this can be so, because truth is there for all to learn; it is just a matter of opening up your consciousness to that capability which is latent within each one of you; the capability of touching the consciousness of one who is there to teach.

Each of you can be a disciple of the truth, attempting to learn the Ancient Wisdom which has been passed down through the millennia to those who have been able to either read books on the subject, or to raise their consciousness to those upon the higher realms, who will give them these truths. There are Masters who can be approached, and We are here to teach all who will learn from Us and We are happy to do this, but there must be an effort made by those upon the Earth to lift their consciousness to that level which We can reach. Once this is done, then We are capable of teaching many things and that seed of truth within will blossom. I hope that you are ready to receive wisdom today. Each one of you has within you the capability of learning many truths; this is evident and has been so since man came upon the Earth. I know that there are books that have great spiritual learning within them. Some of these are extremely intense and concentrated; many too complex for most minds to grasp, but I wish to instil some knowledge of this Ancient Wisdom to those who are interested. My capabilities have been many and varied, and I hope that I can pass on some of this to you.

Most of you are aware that you exist to incarnate many times in order to evolve your soul, and through each incarnation it is hoped that you will learn the truth which you search for; which you have chosen to learn in that incarnation, and to re-educate the mind and soul as time goes by to a higher level, through each time you touch the Earth for a while. In past lives I have incarnated many times, one incarnation of which you may have heard. My name was the Comte de Saint Germaine, and in this lifetime I was part of a brotherhood of men who formed a society of Arcane Wisdom. These men with whom I joined learnt much and we tried to pass on this knowledge to others, but at that time it was not appreciated and many were hunted down and killed because it was thought to be evil. This knowledge that is the truth has often been thought of as evil by those who have closed minds.

It is extremely sad that this should be so, but nevertheless it is. As you know in the past, many high-minded individuals living good lives have been killed in the name of truth. One such was Jesus the Christ, who is also one of the Masters of the Hierarchy as you know, and He was crucified in the name of truth, and yet His name has lived on forever as a Being of perfection, which is the truth. As a result, the teachings that He gave have been passed on through the generations and will be so for ever, because truth will always come to the surface, and you know it to be so. His spirituality shone forth like a beacon of light in the darkness of those days, and He passed on His words to the disciples at that time, for them to continue spreading His word. It is hoped that you as our disciples, will shine forth your spirituality and spread the word to others.

It is difficult to pass on spiritual awareness to those with closed minds. It seems as though that which is most important in your lives; this capability of reaching to higher realms and learning this knowledge of truth is the most difficult thing to pass on to others, unless you find others of like mind with whom you can have speech and compare your learning. You cannot force anything on to those who are unaware of this spirituality, which is there for them to learn. It is latent within everyone, and yet so many seem to be unaware of this all their lives. They are not ready in other words, to receive our words of truth. Perhaps in time they will learn how to meditate and reach up for that knowledge to be given to them. It is hoped that more and more will hear that voice within and act upon it so that this Ancient Wisdom that We the Masters wish to be spread will be learnt by new generations of humanity. Over the centuries we have passed on our knowledge of Arcane Wisdom and we still hope to continue with this work.

When you look back upon your life, have you done all that you can to raise your consciousness to reach upwards? I know that many of you have done so, and are progressing in learning the truth that lies within, but there is still time to improve on your capabilities. If you have life within you, time does not mean much to you until you are older and recognise that you may not have utilised your lives in the best you could have done. It seems when you are younger, that there is plenty of time, and yet you never know, because you can be wrapped up in your own lives and forget that part of you is spiritual.

Time should be made to utilise your capabilities to the full, and to meditate each day, striving to raise your consciousness ever higher. It is a discipline that must be kept. It is so easy to forget that spiritual nature of yours because the world and your life seems more important to you. It cries out to you in a loud voice, whereas your spiritual nature is silent, and the voice that speaks to you from within is very quiet. It is difficult sometimes to remember that part of you, but do so because it is an important part of your lives. I know that perhaps others will think this strange, but if you feel that this is so, keep silent about it and just continue your own learning process because it is important. As you know, as the incarnation passes by, if you have not made this attempt and do not feel that it is important, you will have neglected something that should have been reconciled.

Your life is your responsibility, and your improving of your very soul is your responsibility, because that spirituality within you is that which you are attempting to raise upwards in each incarnation. This information is very important, and you should recognise it as such. Remember that seed of truth within each one of you with which you were born, and allow the flowering of that seed of truth to occur. It is in your spirituality that this will come and you will learn to reach for the Master who will teach you all you need to know; He is the one to whom you should turn for truth to expand. Expand your consciousness so that you can be aware of all who will approach you with the wisdom that you are searching for, but remember always, before you begin that expansion of consciousness to say a prayer of protection, and guidance will be given to you. Jesus said 'I am the way, the truth and the life', and these words that were spoken by Him could have been spoken by any of the Masters of the Hierarchy because We are the way, We are the truth in your lives, and We will guide and comfort you as the time goes by.

When you wish for guidance, raise your consciousness; expand it upwards and outwards, and We will be there to guide you when you have reached Our realm of being. Do not expect it to happen immediately. You can be given guidance by those teachers and guides who are close to you, and eventually they will raise your consciousness so that you can hear the Masters as time goes by. It takes a little while before your consciousness is capable of hearing Our words, but We will be there always. We can come into being upon the Earth when We wish. We do so in certain areas of the world quite constantly, but these are remote areas in high mountainous regions where We meet up and plan strategies of teaching and guidance for humanity. We work together as a team of High Beings, and We try to raise the consciousness of those whom We feel will be able to pass on Our knowledge to others who are of a like mind. We work for the good of humanity, and We are Messengers of Light from God. We are constantly attempting to spread His word to mankind, so that he can become a brotherhood of man throughout the world, instead of being separate parts of the whole. There is so much violence, making separation the norm instead of humanity coming together as a brotherhood uniting in peace and love.

This is what we wish for mankind and we are working towards this end, so that more will come into the light, which we are attempting to spread; light, love and peace throughout the world. We hope that you will become part of this, and We the Masters will continue with Our work regardless of what is happening upon the Earth. We only wish to convey Our own thoughts to those who will listen to Us. We give you our blessing, and I Myself, the Master R, bless you this day and give you peace. God bless, Master Rakoczi

TEACHINGS FROM THE ASCENDED MASTERS-7

You do not need to search for Gurus and Masters far and wide; this is not necessary. Within you, each one of you, there is a great potential and that potential will be realised if you will but have faith in your power; your spiritual power, which is there if you will but learn the capability of reaching upwards; raising your consciousness to that level when the Master will come to you and tell you all that you wish to know. This is possible for all who have the will to do this. We are here and we are reaching out to you; you only have to lift your consciousness towards us. Constantly, We try to give our thoughts, Our wisdom to those upon the Earth, and We have been successful in many cases over the millennia, but it is necessary to be disciplined in your life, spending some time in meditation and upliftment. It is only those who are disciplined in this way who can have the confidence to voice Our words, accept Our thoughts as their own, knowing full well that it is We the Masters who pass on Their knowledge.

Dedication is required, but it does not mean that your whole life is one of meditation, prayer and service. That is only part of your life, but it does help to be in a place of peace for this work, because if there are interruptions and noise surrounding you in a busy disordered life, then it is difficult; almost impossible to do this type of work in order to reach up to Us. If you will try to dedicate part of each day to meditation, then in time you will be able to hear us. We have been helping humanity all the time that mankind has been upon the Earth, and that is Our life; one of service; service to God and man, because We are the mediators from God, sending forth His word to you.

In our lifetimes We have overcome everything that you are attempting to learn; We have been evolving through those incarnations, mastering everything; all the difficulties thrown at Us in those lifetimes, and learning through them. As has been said before, it is only through difficulty that you learn, and through the lifetime in which you exist now, there is much scope because of the raising upward to another dimension. There is an acceleration of everything required for this. Speed is of the utmost importance so that those who are ready to move on to the next dimension must be prepared to work towards this end. No one without dedication will be capable of this. Those who just wish to live in comfort and enjoyment; never thinking of their spiritual nature will not be able to raise up into the fourth dimension, and ultimately the fifth, because it is necessary to attain a certain level of spiritual upliftment.

This Aquarian Age is a time of challenge for all, and it is up to you to accept that challenge within your life. Many have been warning of this Age over the last few decades, but there are so many who are heedless of this, and have just remained static; not accepting any challenges whatsoever. It is rather sad that this must be so, because there are many opportunities for upliftment. Many books abound at present on esoteric subjects, which have been unavailable previously, but they are only for those who have eyes to see and who are on the path to spiritual enlightenment. It is well seen that people will just walk past books of this kind if they are not ready to accept these words of truth. The evolution of your soul can proceed quite quickly if you yourself are ready to accept enlightenment, and this enlightenment can be given in a variety of ways, through reading books, through talking with others of like mind who are already on this path, and through enlightenment from the Masters of the Hierarchy, who are presently helping humanity.

All this can be done from within. You need to have the yearning within you to enable you to work on your capabilities, and as I said previously, this can be achieved through discipline and meditation. We are happy to teach all who are of this mind and We hope that over the time to come, We can help in many ways. It has been said before, that if you will have the faith, miracles can happen, and you will be able to do many things of which you would not have imagined were possible through this faith. Over the centuries miracles have happened to certain individuals, and people have sometimes scoffed at them with disbelief, but others have truly believed in them, and it is through them that they have been raised to be Saints or Avatars over the years that have passed.

There are living Avatars at present; for instance, Mother Meera in Germany is a living example of this. As you know, an Avatar is a reincarnation of a Deity, and they have proved through their lives that they are shining examples of this. Sai Baba of course performs miracles daily as proof for those who need these examples of His power. He produces vibhuti constantly, which has great power within it for healing, and apart from vibhuti that forms in His hands, it has been shown to be possible that vibhuti can form on photographs of him in people's homes, just to prove that he has been present in that house. He can be omnipresent, and this proves that miraculous happenings are occurring all the time if people will have the faith. Sai Baba also produces artefacts within His hands, small photos, amulets or beads which people can keep to prove that he is a living example of one who can perform miracles.

Over the centuries, being such as these have been examples to all to show that mankind can do more than he does if he will raise his spirituality to a much higher level than he has done. I know that certain beings have great powers within them from an early age, but even so, everyone has within them that spark of divinity that can be fanned to a flame, so that all can do many more things than they would ever imagine within their lives. The power and capability is given to them from God, and this capability can be nurtured if you have the will, and particularly so at this time when transition into the fourth dimension will be occurring with the next decade, so that mankind will be becoming more spiritual in body, and will be able to see many things of which at present he is unable. Beings which abound upon the Earth which are in the fourth and fifth dimension, and which eventually man will be able to see quite clearly, and this would be considered a miracle, or if not a miracle, a phenomenon of great power, but it will be occurring more and more frequently as the veil thins between the two dimensions, and so it will be that man will be capable of seeing spirit which is dwelling around him.

So many of you think of spiritual beings as being above you in heaven as you call it, but spirit is all around you. Beings from higher realms are here to help mankind constantly. Your guides and teachers are here, and although you feel that you must look upwards to them, it is just in a manner of speaking, because you have to raise your consciousness up to them and therefore you think that they dwell above you, but it is just a level of consciousness really. In actual fact, the Devic Kingdom is also going to be visible to you in time to come. Therefore you will see many beings of light that are invisible at present. You too are beings of light, but perhaps not as bright as the Angelic Beings. The Devas, the large Devas who cover great tracts of the Earth are Beings of Light and Power, and they are beautiful to see as are all the Angelic Beings. In time to come, you will be able to see them all, but at present, as you know, they can be there and heard by certain of you, but you cannot see them unless they choose to show themselves to you in some way.

Know that you have the potential within you to develop that clear sightedness even now, so that you will be able to see much if you will work on this. As I said at the beginning, all of you have potential within you, if you have the faith and discipline to develop this potential in many ways. So that if you wish to see and hear, you can try to develop your third eye area, which will open in time to come, and then you will have the capability which is latent. You will see symbols, and in time to come, Beings of Light. I hope that I give you all that you wish to learn because there is so much for mankind to look forward to in the future in this respect. He will be capable of learning many things over the next few years if he has the will to do so. There is much more opportunity at present than there has been for decades, and it is only a question of having the faith and the will to learn, and you will spread your wings and be aware of great things over the next few years. We will teach you all you wish to know, and We send the Blessing of God this day to all of you. God Bless, Master Rakoczi.

TEACHINGS FROM THE ASCENDED MASTERS-8

We the Masters of the Hierarchy wish to help to restore God's plan on Earth. As you say in the Great Invocation, 'Let light and love and power restore the Plan on Earth'; and this is our work. We are attempting through humanity, to restore that Plan; to spread God's Word and His wishes to as many as we can. There are evil and violent men who are wreaking havoc throughout certain parts of the world at present, but in time this havoc will be restored to normal life, and peace will reign once more. We know that in your hearts, this too is your wish for all men, and that the Earth herself will be restored and made green and pleasant once again. The Earth has been suffering too as a result of man's exploitations, but it seems that sense is being restored, and people are becoming aware of what has been done to the Earth over the last few decades, and there are attempts to stop pollution, or at least it is being modified considerably over the last few years.

As you know, many television programmes have been made to attempt to make man feel guilt about his treatment of the Earth, because so much has been done to destroy the natural habitat, both for animal and bird life, and for natural growth of tree, plant and hedgerow, and the whole Earth herself has been completely exploited to the furthest extent possible. Now man has seen his result and has begun to replant, re-forest the Earth and stop pollution. It is well past the normal time for this, and we hope that the Earth itself will recover. It will take some doing because so many rivers and seas have become overpolluted, and the natural fish and birds who frequent these areas have been devastated. In time, things will improve, but time must be given for the natural creatures of the wild to restore their numbers, so man must hold his hand and prevent further exploitation of these beautiful creatures. There have been great attempts made by groups such as Greenpeace, to make many countries understand what they are doing to the seas of the world. So many have just continued their greedy exploitations of the oceans and have made the numbers dwindle to a miserable extent, and have over fished and killed great creatures of the deep in their power and hunger. Sadly this has caused great disruption of the natural balance of nature, but given time, as I say, all will return to normal numbers, but it will take a few years before this happens.

We hope that mankind will understand what has occurred since he existed upon the Earth. From the first, man had no reasoning of what might occur in the hundreds and thousands of years of his existence in the future, and therefore when he first began life upon the Earth, there was no thought of the future. For instance, when the Egyptian civilisation began, and man first built the Pyramids, and lived upon a beautiful fertile plain, there was no thought of what would happen when the trees were denuded; no thought of what would happen when he over-cultivated those plains of Egypt and eroded the

Earth. In time, of course, it became a desert area, with only the very bare minimum of fertile land near the Nile. The rest of Egypt had been supplanted with sand, and sadly that has been the way of it for millennia. This has happened throughout the whole of the Earth, because originally the Earth was fertile and clothed with green; trees, bushes and grass, and all manner of beautiful flowers. Sadly, over those millennia man has taken toll of so many areas which have been denuded of forest, and although it could not have been foreseen in the early days, latterly, he has just proceeded without thought, and as a result the Earth has suffered.

In future times the Earth will restore herself, and man will have more thought towards what he does to the green and fertile land, and I know that humanity has thoughts of helping the Earth now, and thoughts of helping one another which is part of God's Plan for mankind. So much has been done by those who have money to help those Third World countries who have been starving and have had so much suffering, with famine and drought in certain areas which are parched and becoming desert-like, but eventually there will be a balance made, and the whole of the Earth will be temperate in time to come, so that those areas which at present are parched will have normal rainfall, sufficient to keep them in food, and other parts which are colder will be more equable and will be able to cope without so much heating as you do at present. Things will balance out, so that the whole of the Earth will be pleasant to live in, and humanity itself will feel more able to live together as brothers instead of fighting one another.

Mankind was put upon the Earth to act in brotherly love to one another, but how often has this occurred? Not for very long at a time, but in time to come there is much to look forward to, and mankind will change in his attitude, and be as one, attempting to live in harmony upon the Earth. United; acting in a Christian manner to one another and to all things. All animal life will be treated with concern and fellowship instead of slaughtering those who would be man's friend. Animals have been killed for food for so long, but gradually; slowly but surely, there will be a change in man's attitude, particularly when they themselves realise that animals too have within them a divinity, and they too have a right to live upon the Earth as man does.

As time goes by, and the Earth and everything upon it gradually rises upwards into a higher dimension of being, with that, ascending into a higher dimension, man's mind will come to a new understanding of what life is meant to be about. His purpose for being here; for learning in so many different ways, and his attitude towards both other men and animal life will change completely. It may be that before this rise into the fourth and fifth dimensions there will be some disruption upon the Earth. There may be changes come about upon the Earth's surface, and with that, there will be some who will return to spirit; who are not suitable to rise upwards into the fourth dimension; those men of violence of whom I spoke at the beginning. It will be a time to sort out the sheep from the goats as was said in the Bible, and those who have become strong in evil will be taken away. You will be protected; those of you who walk in the light and are on the path of spiritual development. Those who have attempted to do their best in their lifetime and to reach upwards towards the light will be under God's protection and care. He will see that His loved ones are given every protection available, and all will be well for you and yours when this time approaches. So never fear, you will be the chosen people who will inherit the Earth when she rises upwards to that higher dimension of which I spoke.

It is difficult to say when these changes will come about. Several people have told you before of these changes. It has been mentioned by the Master Jesus, and by those who have spoken to you from other planets, so do not concern yourselves about this. You will be looked after by us, the Masters, and also by those who are protecting you from any other worlds. Beings from many planets who have been watching over the Earth for some time. Changes have already begun occurring in your climate and in your being. They will be gradual, and some of you may be aware already of these changes, but all will come to pass in good time and We will be here for guidance, so if you wish to ask questions on this topic We will be happy to answer you at any time. You may tell others about this phenomenon which will be occurring over the next few years, but do not mention it to those who are not ready to receive these thoughts. You yourselves can weigh up who are the best to accept this message. In the meantime, be of good cheer and We will be with you at all times. God bless and keep you now and always, Master Rakoczi.

TEACHINGS FROM THE ASCENDED MASTERS-9

We, the Masters of the Hierarchy serve God and humanity equally. Naturally, our service to God is all-important, and we hope that in time to come that all of humanity will have a similar outlook to serve God and humanity, and as a result, be as one with us and also be of one accord, thereby creating a new Earth, as it was revealed in the Bible – 'There shall be a new Heaven and a new Earth', and in this, mankind can create a new life. In a short space of time it is hoped that this new life will begin. Once you have reached a higher level of consciousness and being, then this new beginning will be fulfilled. In a short space of time in earthly terms, this new start will be created; from out of the ashes, the phoenix will arise, and there will be no more violence and evil, because once that phoenix arises, light will have descended on the Earth, and God's Plan will come to pass. The door will be closed to evil and humanity will be renewed; he will be as he was once before when he walked and talked with God and the Angelic Hierarchy.

As you already know, there are changes upon the Earth, and new energies are working in order to help mankind to adjust to the changes in frequency upon the Earth. Some may be quite acutely aware of this, whereas others have noticed no difference and continue their day-to-day existence unaware of anything that is due to happen in future days. This is where those upon the spiritual path can help others to understand what will be occurring in the future, and ready them for these changes that will be happening. As you know, mankind is ready to rise to the fourth and fifth dimension, and when that occurs, he will be able to see and hear much more than at present. I am talking now of those who are both in the spiritual realms, and those who exist on other worlds who have been, as you know, helping the Earth, and those who dwell upon it to adjust to a new way of thinking and living. They exist on the fifth dimension, and have done so for a great number of years. It matters not how long; it just matters for you to know that there are many 'out there' as you might say, helping or ready to help. They too serve God, and many beings, both humanity and beings on other worlds who are also changing their circumstances like yourselves. So, as well as the Masters, there are beings who have good intention and serve God and humanity, and others like ourselves.

We have incarnated many times, and through those incarnations, have learnt much; existing to evolve and improve the soul. We have mastered all things; everything that has been thrown at us, shall we say; troubles, sickness, conditions; everything that man is heir to, we have managed to control, and improve our souls in each incarnation, and as a result we have been aware of what you have had to cope with in this lifetime. Many people throughout the world have been suffering over these last few decades, and we understand everything that is happening. It is the Age of Kali, and you must undergo this evil and Dark Age before you come into the light, of the Golden Age when you will find peace and men will live together as one.

At present you cannot imagine this occurring, and most of you understand that you must go through a worse condition before this new Golden Age comes about. But it will happen; this is prophesied, and has been ordained for some time, and you are privileged to be here at this time of change.

You have chosen to incarnate here and now in order to create calm out of chaos, and to help others to understand and bring them into that new way of thinking, otherwise those who cannot comprehend or wish to comprehend what must happen before this new beginning starts, then they will not be part of this new order. Those who are not ready to understand or cope with the changes, as you know will die to this incarnation and not rise upwards into the fourth, and ultimately the fifth dimensions. They will go to spirit and then return to a third dimensional planet until they are ready to accept this new order, and they will return to the Earth when they are ready in the following incarnation. To be of service to one another is a wonderful thing, and to serve God is a glory that we understand, and we have always wished to serve throughout our lifetimes. It is only those who do not follow the path of spirituality who do not necessarily feel this way. It is hoped that you who are reading this communication will feel as we do, that you wish to serve humanity as well as you can through your service to God.

Mankind having free will, is unlike the Angelic Hierarchy, in that they do not necessarily serve God, but the Angelic Hierarchy are here to serve. That is their purpose, to serve God and do whatever he wishes. Perhaps mankind will on his ascendancy to higher vibratory levels become as one with the Angels and wish to serve constantly also; We the Masters have been thinking this for some time. As you know, it was quoted in the Bible that man is a little lower than the Angels, and perhaps from now on, once he has raised into that higher dimension, he will have the same attitude as the Angels, and have less of his free will in his nature; less egotistical and more brotherly love, unconditional love for his fellow man. We have been hoping over this last decade that changes would come about in those countries where dictatorship, violence and religious wars have been occurring throughout this time; throughout time immemorial for that matter. But we have been hoping that from now on this will come to an end, and that those who have the wish to serve as the World Servers, will manage to alter other men's thinking through sending out light and love each day, as many of you already do. Perhaps in time this will take a more powerful effect on those places where darkness still prevails, and we too have come to play our part in sending forth the light to these dark places.

I, the Master R, and many of the other Masters have spent many decades in and out of incarnation. We have served humanity in this way, and we exist in high mountainous regions, usually in the Himalayas or the Andes. These areas are ideal for our purpose, and we are part of the White Brotherhood. It is one and the same thing, which many of you may know, and we hope that through our appearing to man from time to time, and being near humanity we feel that in this way we can serve God's purpose better than if we were completely in the spiritual realms. Therefore, our service to God is rather different from that of the Angels who are always in the spiritual realms, and we hope that in the future when you see us face to face, that you too will try to emulate us in your lives once this new beginning; this Golden Age has taken effect.

Within each one of you there is a mighty divine power from the Source of all being, which is there to be utilised for the good of others. Some of you are partially aware of it, but most are not; it is a latent power to be used to channel both communication from the Realms of Light, and to send forth healing through touch or through thought. This great power is to be used in serving God; as I said, for the good of others and will be of great use at the time of the Earth changes and beyond. It can only be used in love and compassion, and in the need to communicate God's Word. A wonderful new life will begin for all of you in future days. There is so much for you to look forward to, and for your children and your children's children. Life will be so different, but it is all up to you yourselves to do what you can at this time, and we will guide you through this time and help you towards the light. I give my blessing to you and all who will read this communication.

God bless and keep you, Master Rakoczi.

TEACHINGS FROM THE ASCENDED MASTERS-10

I wish to speak today on reincarnation. This subject is one that is shown much interest in these days, and I know that you yourselves have been reading over the past years about the subject. In my various incarnations, I have experienced quite a number that have proved important and informative to others. The first of these was Hermes Trismegistus who has been the basis of many teachings; it was at his instigation that a number of affirmations were made; Cosmic Laws you might call them, and various religions were based on these. This is something that I cannot claim to be truly responsible for myself; although it was my soul that incarnated, I of myself feel completely distanced from this because it was so long ago in past history. Nevertheless, these Cosmic Laws, which were founded at that time, have been used over thousands of years as a basis, and I think that they are still in use now. It was at my; I say my in loose terms; my instigation that various laws were laid down at that time. Many of you have heard of Hermetic philosophy, and this was based on these laws; I will not go into great detail because it is not necessary at this time, but I know that some of you are aware that this incarnation was truly an important one.

I have incarnated at many times in the history of man, and have helped to form several important sects that began new thoughts on religion and the power of thought. One of these was the Rosicrucians, and I know that they are still in existence even now. It is an arcane sect and is kept from the general public because of its exclusivity. It was when I was Francis Bacon in the sixteenth to early seventeenth centuries, in the reign of Elizabeth the First that this came into being. I wrote many books and teachings, given through inspiration at that time, and I was able to form groups of people who were dedicated to the uplifting of mankind's consciousness. In those days it was difficult to do anything of this kind unless it was secret, because if it became known to the general public then there would be a great outcry and we would be designated as a group of black magicians that we were not; in fact it was more white magic that we were dabbling in. We were not magicians; we were only trying to raise our divinity to the highest possible, and to try and spread the word of God in a different way from the normal religions of that time.

In these days it is easier for humanity to do this because unless you are Royalty or well known figures, then it is possible to form groups of like minded people like you yourselves have done, in order to have people come to talk on various subjects allied to spirituality. In those days I was a well-known figure and it was difficult to do this type of work even in an arcane way. Thus it was very exclusive, and there were vows to be taken, rather like the masons, so that it was all secret to the general public, and these vows had to be kept at that time, and in fact I think that the Rosicrucian Order is still exclusive, and I believe it is quite costly to join. I am not certain of this, but in those days it certainly was, and as a result, it has always been maintained as a secret order, but something that was important to develop at that time. I think that those who followed have maintained this order very well.

In history books I was linked with the Royal Family, and I was truly a part of it; of noble birth, and my incarnation then I think was also an important one. You too may have been in the past royal, or linked with royalty, but this matters not because once you return to spirit all are the same. You may be aware that although I am presently the Master R, I was in the past also the Comte de Saint Germaine, and I existed for a great number of years in that particular incarnation, which created a mystery at that time for some in the European Courts, but I was able to do some good for others in existence then.

I feel that I must talk about others rather than purely my own incarnations, and I know that all of you from time to time have had incarnations which have been important to yourselves and those around you, because all of you on the path to spirituality have in the past probably been Atlanteans. Also, you will have had Egyptian and Grecian incarnations as part of a temple group; either Priests or Priestesses, in order to lead you to this interest in your spirituality now; and to be so far along the path so that you can absorb this work and have an open mind on the subject of your own divinity. It is important at this time as I said, because as you know, you will be rising upwards to higher dimensions in the near future, and it will be much easier for you to do this if your consciousness is maintained on a high level. This must be through meditation daily; twice daily if possible, in order to keep the level at a high standard.

I know that some of you have very busy lives and it may be difficult to fit this type of work into your lives, but believe me, it is an important part of your life. Do not think that the physical life is all-important. You must maintain the spirituality because basically, man is spirit, and that side of his nature is just as important as the physical. You are in a physical body in order to experience life on Earth, but that life is twofold, because your spiritual nature must evolve through each incarnation. It is only when you are in incarnation that you will find that you can learn so much more, experiencing many situations that could not be possible in the spirit world. Your past experiences will enable you to understand this, and to remember if you can what you learnt at that time. I know that when you come to this Earth you wonder why you are here and what you have to learn, but realise that the result of past incarnations is built into this one, and make the most of it, using this life to its utmost. You have the ability to reach up and inwards to hear what God and other High Beings have to inform you in your future. Recognise this and try to listen with that inner ear each day.

As you practice meditation, you will find that you can control your thoughts and experience more in hearing through inspiration from those in the spirit world, or if you cannot hear, seeing symbols which will convey meaning to you as you learn to discover what they mean. At times you may think; I can see a chalice or a beautiful light which turns into another shape, and which may symbolise something of great importance. Try to find out what these symbols and lights mean, because if you cannot hear, as some people cannot, the light and symbol can mean just as much as words do to others. Truth will be given to you if you will close out the outer world. Just a little time each day, linking with your higher self is the most important time of the day for all of you.

All are attempting to evolve their souls to a higher level of being, and when the spirit returns home to the source, he becomes one with us all. He tries to do his best in his lifetime, and that is all that can be done. Attempting to do good, to rise to a higher spirituality, attempting to fan that little spark which is in each one of you to become an incandescent flame. That light within will become a great flame if you will allow it to, and you can learn so much if you will listen within to that still small voice. Life on Earth is for learning, it is also for enjoyment, and it is a challenge to all of you. I hope that perhaps I may have helped you in some way in this communication. Believe me I did not wish to bore you with details of my incarnations, but just wished you to know that all of you have had your important times, if not important now. I know that you all are striving to improve in many ways, and I hope to help you in this.

God bless and keep you all, Master Rakoczi.

TEACHINGS FROM THE ASCENDED MASTERS-11

The Masters of the Hierarchy are at present trying to help mankind to realise his full potential. I know that you have been attempting to do all things possible to raise your consciousness. Many of you have been meditating for years and feel that you have done all that you can, and although you wish that you could do more, it is difficult for you to recognise the fact that man is capable of very much more and will be reaching his potential in the time to come. Recognise the fact that you are spirit, which you know, enclosed in a physical being, but your spirit has been incarnating very many times, and has more potential than you can realise.

You know that spiritual beings such as Devas are of great size. They are fountains of light as they have described themselves to you, and this is very true. All different colours; some are silver and blue tones; great fountains of beautiful colours; others are rainbow colours and some are colours of fire; all streaming if you could see them, into the air and around perhaps twenty or thirty feet in size. Now, if you think of a human being, and the size of him, perhaps between five and six feet roughly, but that is nothing like the size of that being of light. Each of you has around you your aura and that is filled with light, and the aura can extend great distances, depending on the experience of that soul. Great beings such as Avatars have auras that extend tremendous distances, but each one of you has, apart from the aura, that light streaming from within, which projects upwards quite extensively and surrounds you, extending beyond the aura, and the aura is variable depending on the mood of the person or the experience, as I have said.

Visualise, each of you have surrounding you and from within, this wonderful light projecting around and integrating with each others' auras and light, so if we gaze down from above at mankind, there are lights projecting everywhere. It is like looking down on fountains of light shining upwards and filling the whole of the atmosphere above you. You cannot imagine how beautiful it is, and you are completely unaware of this; you only think of beings of light as the Angelic Beings or the Masters which we are, but you yourselves are beautiful beings of light if you did but know. This is something which we feel you should be aware of and to try to recognise this factor, bringing it into your daily life so that you can think of yourselves as light, and try to recognise this within each person that you meet. Try to think of each of you as being a part of God, which you are. Think of yourselves each day as being spirit; a part of God, and then you will always be protected.

This is a new thought perhaps for some of you, and I know that you have been aware that you are divine sparks, but if you think of each one of you shining forth that light, then you must realise that it is important that you encourage that light and be God in your being; your very soul, and think of your life extending behind you and forwards, and think of that future extending and improving your life by the very thought of that projection of light which is you. Perhaps in meditation you could reach upwards more, reaching into the realms of light, and using light to bring you into a higher consciousness, using your super consciousness extensively, and recognising the fact that you can connect with God each time you meditate; not just occasionally, and learn quicker than you have ever done if you will try to improve this ability each day. We have been attempting to guide mankind for many centuries; so long that we cannot tell you but that matters not. It only matters that you yourselves realise your capabilities and improve upon them.

We are always close to the Earth at this time of year because of the joy and hope for future days at Easter time; recognising the fact of the resurrection, and we know that you believe in this, and believe in the life to come, and the many lifetimes after that which man has had since the resurrection. We know that each one of you has hope in your hearts because of this time of year, and the season that goes with it because of nature bringing forth its fruitfulness.

The beauty of the flowers and the sunshine, the buds appearing; new growth burgeoning everywhere, and it is hoped that there will be new growth in the hearts of men and that the love and light that you can project to one another will spread to those areas which have been besieged by violence; where terror stalks and we wish that those people will be given comfort and recognise that the hope they have will reign throughout the world. The peace that can be given to all men is a joyous thing, and if at all possible each day, try to project that light from within you towards all those areas where there is violence and there has been chaos for a number of years. Think positively and with the knowledge that all will be well in future times when the Golden Age comes, and the promise of God's Plan for man will be fulfilled.

The Masters are sending forth powerful energies to the Earth at this time, and we have great hopes for mankind for the future. He is capable of so much love; unconditional love which has been bottled up within. Try to allow that love and light to flow forth from you, so that all can be enveloped in that love, and then no man can turn his hand against another; if the power of that love is strong enough, it will always prevail against evil. We feel that evil has been having its time upon the Earth of recent years, but those days are numbered, and light will overcome this darkness if you yourselves will help us in this work, and project light constantly to those places where evil has been reigning. I know that many of you have been doing this for some time, but the more people who will join in this dedication of themselves to lifting darkness from the Earth, then the quicker it will happen, and love and light will prevail. We ourselves have been working on this, and many Beings of Light have been attempting to raise men's consciousness and consciences so that they will become better people to control events upon the Earth.

Man has ruled all the kingdoms of the Earth. He has dominion over the animals, the plants and the minerals, and it is his responsibility for the Earth herself; she has been suffering with much which has occurred over many years, such as pollution and devastation of vast forests, but mankind is learning and we have hope that all will be put to rights. Much reforestation is occurring now, and man is attempting to right the wrongs that he has caused upon the Earth, and the seas and rivers are gradually recovering from the pollution that has been wrought upon them. As I said, we have great hopes for mankind for the future, and we know that in time to come, he will realise his potential and all become true beings of light. We give you our blessing this day. I, the Master R in particular have great hope, and I know that in time to come, you will all realise what you are, and what you are capable of.

God bless, Master Rakoczi.

TEACHINGS FROM THE ASCENDED MASTERS-12

Remember always, your time on Earth is precious. Do not squander that time. It is important that whatever comes into your life as a challenge is faced and dealt with, as well as you possibly can. At times you may feel rather tired and cannot be concerned with others, but remember too that some are not aware that they have the ability to work with light. This is important; use Light from God in your lives to send forth love; unconditional love to all. This is where those on the spiritual path have the benefit that others may not have, and spread this light to them.

Each incarnation is important to you because it is an opportunity for your soul to evolve a little higher each time. Do not think that it is important to concern yourself with past lives; those are past history now. You may have been important in some of those lives either historically or as a person who gave life to others, or helped them medically by dealing with injuries, or instructing them through education. This is not important now, because each life you return a better soul or should be. It is your opportunity to excel in whatever you can do well, and learn each time you return; remember, this may be your last opportunity to evolve higher with that soul.

As a Master I am well aware of the frailties of man and I know how difficult it is at times to turn the other cheek and to deal with triumph and disaster, and as Kipling said, 'treat those two imposters just the same'. There are times when you feel that you cannot prevail against disaster, but know that you are never alone. Remember that God is always with you, and He can help you at all times. Have faith and believe in yourself; it is important that you do this and then you can prevail against anything. You will have a strong knowing that you are working with the Light. Breathe in the Light of the living God; see it before you and breathe it into every cell of your body, so that you are filled with light and exude that light around you, protecting yourself against all ills and no harm can befall you. Instruct others that they may learn this, and by this method, you can raise your consciousness to a higher level in meditation. In this way no evil can befall, and those beings who come to you with love, and will give forth their teachings to you. Always allow that quiet time of the day when you raise your consciousness to receive instruction and communication with the Realms of Light. Sometimes God will speak to you, sometimes your guide or another Being of Light, but always you will receive benefit of some kind that will give you strength for the day, and you will learn as time goes by how powerful these thoughts can be in your life.

These are momentous days in the lives of men. At this time in the history of man there are powerful energies abroad. We the Masters and others from the Realms of Light are pouring forth these energies to man in order that he may evolve much faster in these latter days. It was foretold that mankind would find himself at this time. There have been times in the past when mankind has shown himself for what he is; a child of Light, and now you have the opportunity to become true children of Light; children of God, and act as He would wish you to act, prevailing against the darkness within the world at this time. Sending forth His Light to all areas where violence is occurring, and with God's help, all this will come to pass, and the darkness will be overcome by light. We, the Masters have great faith in man and his capabilities, and know that We ourselves overcame darkness in this way, and you too can prevail against the darkness and evil.

Two thousand years have gone by since Jesus the Christ walked the Earth, and as a Master, He was aware of the evil in those men's' hearts who prevailed against Him. He knew that this was His destiny, and that man would eventually see the error of his ways. He was aware that others would take up the Light that He carried and prevail against that darkness. He knew that the Light of God would come to mankind through His destiny of the Crucifixion, and that in the future He would be known as the true bringer of Light to the Earth. He works with us even now as Sananda, as he is known. All Masters of the Light have been working with the Angelic forces for many years, but now of all times, the power is becoming stronger and many of you sense this power upon the Earth and within you. The energies are becoming stronger and we are helping man to realise his potential; he can become a greater being of Light than he is at present. All of you are able to pour forth energies of light to the Earth, to others; to all who live upon the Earth, and you can send forth healing power to one another. There is great potential within each one of you if you will learn how to use this power from God.

Each one of you was made in the image of God, and when life began on Earth, when man first came into being, he was constantly in touch with God and the Angelic forces. This has been lost through the ages, but it is returning and you are capable of being in touch constantly in order to send forth healing wherever you wish. This capability is latent within each one of you, but believe me, you have great power potential for healing and love, if you will but free this capability and allow it to flow forth freely from within. Reach upwards and allow God's healing power to flow through you as a channel of light, and all can be achieved if you have the faith. You know that a mother can pick up a child who has fallen and hurt his knee and rub it, and the child feels better at once. This is healing in its simplest form, but extend it to others and the same thing can occur.

All this is given to you, and it needs only to be awakened within each one of you. There are many of you who are already capable of healing others, but it is there latent within everyone, and this is something that is important to know, and to awaken it in all, so that this capability can be shared throughout the world to all men.

In this last communication with you, I would like to give an Invocation to the Light, for some of you to use whenever you feel that this would be advisable. It will be something which you will remember easily; a simple Invocation to the Light.

> "Wielder of the Sword of Light come forth.
> Defend man from his darkness.
> May God's pure Divine Light shine through the hearts of men,
> And love and peace prevail."

It is a simple Invocation, but one that I feel will be quite powerful in time to come. In asking for Michael the Archangel to come forth, there will be power given, as He is the defender of the Lord; He will prevail against any darkness. He has been helping for many years. The whole of the Earth is dependent upon him for this Light that has been given since God sent his Son to the Earth, and I know that you are aware that this love that was brought through the Light is within the hearts of all men if it can be prevailed upon to shine forth to others.

What is required now is your faith and your help in this work of the Masters. We have been sending to all of you Our love, and We know that many of you have been light workers for some time. We ask that you continue in this work, and We know that all of you will do your best to bring others into this work for future days. We have faith in you, and I know that you will do your utmost to join with Me in this work.
God bless and keep you all, now and always,
Master Rakoczi.

FOR THOSE NEW TO CHANNELLING

For anyone who has not so far heard of channelling I shall explain about it here.

Channelling normally occurs after the recipient has become accustomed to meditating regularly, and is a form of message taking from higher realms.

During meditation, he or she is used to listening to that still small voice within, not really a voice, but thoughts that are dropped into the mind by their guide or, eventually, a higher being such as an angel or master.

There is normally a signal given, such as a slight pressure on the top of the head, which is what I experienced, as a sign to take notice, and to still any random thoughts and listen within.

The Ascended Masters are souls who have incarnated many times and overcome every difficulty experienced by mankind, and triumphed over all adversities that man is heir to.

They have become true Masters of everything, and only wish to help mankind in whatever way they can.

They are members of the White Brotherhood, who exist mainly in spirit form, and who gather in a remote area of the Himalayas, and other remote places around the world.

TEACHINGS

FROM THE

ASCENDED MASTERS

PART TWO

TEACHINGS FROM THE MASTERS
Book Two

CONTENTS   Page

Section 1 – Master Jesus/Sananda	48
Section 2 – Master Jesus/Sananda	51
Section 3 – Master Jesus/Sananda	54
Section 4 – Master Jesus/Sananda	57
Section 5 – Master Jesus/Sananda	60
Section 6 – Master Rakoczi	63
Section 7 – Master Rakoczi	66
Section 8 – Master Rakoczi	69
Section 9 – Master Rakoczi	72
Section 10 – Master Rakoczi	75
Section 11 – Master Rakoczi	78
Section 12 – Master Rakoczi	81

Channelled by Beryl Charnley

TEACHINGS FROM THE MASTERS-1

I am He, Light of the World. You have known Me for so long as Master Jesus, but long ago the name of Sananda was conferred upon Me as one of the three Kumaras who serve under Sanat Kumara – Lord of the World. This honour was given and I was pleased to accept and I have been working under this name for long years. It is only of comparatively recent times that it became known that it was I who was now called Sananda. It may be strange to you that for so long I have been in this situation, and it was not known upon the Earth except by a very few. It matters not to Me, but I know that you may like to pass on this knowledge to others that they may also be aware of it and choose to call me Sananda if they wish. I am happy to be known by either name, but strangely enough it is much easier to be known as Sananda. It has been My honour to act as one of the Kumaras for all this time. As you are aware, all Beings of Light are gradually attempting to improve and evolve their souls to a higher level. I too am attempting to do this work and so gradually all of us are attempting to come nearer to the Godhead, towards the Trinity.

God the Father has always wished His children to strive to their utmost and to evolve their souls slowly but surely over the centuries, so that they come closer towards His throne. You yourselves are attempting to improve your capabilities, and I know in time to come, you will be eventually rewarded. It all takes time and experience, and those Masters of the Hierarchy who have evolved their souls to as high level as they can, are always rewarded for their work and for their dedication. The Lord of the World who is the Ancient of Days is based in Shambhala, which is on the etheric level of course, but it is known to all of you who are on the spiritual path. It is towards this area that you all attempt to send your energies when sending forth healing towards the world, because it is a powerful place around the area above the Gobi desert, as you know. You will find that as time goes by, the energies from all the prayers and thoughts of humanity are guided from this area towards those places, which need light sent towards them, and love and light will prevail in time to come.

I will always be working for the good of humanity because that is My wish; to serve mankind always, and I also work with those from other planets, other beings of light who are also attempting to help mankind at this time in these latter days. They are important days for man and you will find, I am sure you have already, that your capabilities of reaching upwards to the Realms of Light are improving, and you are finding that you can channel energies and communications easier now, because all these Beings of Light are pouring forth their healing energies and love to mankind from both their space craft and the planets. Obviously the energies from the planets are dispersed somewhat, but they do gradually filter through towards the Earth.

Those who are in the space craft around the Earth are joining with Me in the work involved at present; that of helping mankind in this transition stage before reaching up to the fifth dimension. There are many beings who are joining forces with Myself, amongst them the Archangel Michael, who has always been at My right hand so to speak, helping with the Angelic Hierarchy to bring light down onto the Earth and counteract the darkness, bringing mankind into the light, and sending his love and Our love to enable the forces of evil to be completely dispersed and then man can come into his own.

As you know, the Masters of the Hierarchy have been working together for so long to help mankind. They come and go as the need arises, so that they dwell both in the Realms of Light and from time to time, come into being upon the Earth. You are aware that the Masters have mankind at heart and only wish to serve. There are a number of people who wish to bring about a change within the hearts of men, and they have been serving the Masters at a very high level. There are certain Avatars who at present are incarnating and they are bringing about changes. One such is Mother Meera in German, to whom many have come and felt her power and love fill them, and returned refreshed and renewed. She has accomplished great things and has changed the lives of many throughout Europe and other Continents throughout the world. Another of course is Sai Baba at Bangalore in India. He has served the Indian continent, and so many have come from all over the world to visit his ashram at Puttaparti. He has created miracles which have been necessary for certain people who would not perhaps have believed him without these miraculously produced gifts, and he also produces vibhuti, which can be used to heal. It is something, which can only be produced by an Avatar, a very High Being, and this sacred ash has saved many lives over the years that he has been working there.

There are other beings of power who are incarnating at present, who are helping man to raise his thoughts so he becomes aware that it is possible for many things to be done, which he would not have thought feasible, but humanity is capable of so much more than he imagines. You are all beings of light; some of you have auras, which spread far further than you would imagine. The Avatars of course have auras that spread for miles around them and include everyone who is within the area of the aura, so that all will benefit from the divinity that shines forth. All of you have that divinity in you. You know that God is within each one of you and that he can do all things, so that through Him you too can do all things if you wish to.

You are aware that thought is most powerful, for thoughts are things, so always guard your thoughts. Do not ever wish ill upon anyone because it might come to pass and you would regret it. Always send forth powerful thoughts of love and healing and then no ill will befall people through you, only goodness will prevail. Always when I incarnated as Jesus, I sent forth love and compassion, and through this there is healing. Always have compassion in your hearts for others, even if you are ill used by them, always keep love within you. It is difficult at times to turn the other cheek, but remember that whatever you send forth that you too will reap rather like Karma, as you sow so shall you reap. So it does not pay to send forth evil thoughts or wish misfortune on another, because it could befall you eventually, although it is not with that thought in mind that you should send forth love. It should come naturally, springing up from the heart.

The Lord of the World, Sanat Kumara, is filled with love for all beings, and he has conferred great love upon Me, and the other two Kumaras with whom I work, Sanaka and Sanatana. We work together and spend much time with humanity. It is not known that We are around, because we can be sending energies and love towards all of you, and you may not be aware of this, but this does not matter to us, We just send our power where it is required, so that there are changes in the thoughts of men. You will find that in time this power will take effect, and there will be less violence and more love and peace throughout the world. We help to guide the Masters in the work they do, and in time to come there will be more who will be more than just men. They will gradually become Masters through the evolvement of the soul, but it all takes time and experience, and we will do what we can to help you all, and guide you as time goes by within the next few years. The changes that will come to you and the Earth will be gradual, and we will make it easy for you to ascend to that higher dimension of being. In the meantime, I give you My great love and blessings to each one of you.

God bless, Sananda.

TEACHINGS FROM THE MASTERS-2

I am happy to greet you; this is Sananda. This is a time of change for all humanity; change is all around you and this is good. Without change there would be no growth, and you must grow into the light, which has been sent down to the Earth to expand and fill each one of you, God's Divine Light. You will find that as time goes by, you will feel stronger and be able to be in contact with those beings of light who wish to communicate with you. Each one of you is rising gradually, slowly but surely into a higher vibratory level. This is necessary at this time and should be a natural process, part of the Earth changes that are occurring at this time. The Earth herself is gradually changing, but you may not be aware of anything. It is not necessary to be aware of the change, only go with the flow and allow it to happen to you. We are here to guide you and we will take care of everything. The Masters have always obeyed Our wish. I too was a Master until I became a Kumara, but even so, I continue to be a Master and join with those who visit the Earth constantly.

As you know, I am here to serve humanity always. It is part of My work for God, and My plan is that humanity will feel no great discomfort as these changes continue, and you will rise into the fifth dimension as time goes by. Over the next few years it will be a gradual process, and We hope that when you have reached that high level of being, you will find that life is wonderful. It will certainly be different for you, you have been told in the past that man will be a co-creator with God and this is so. Once you have gained the fifth dimension you will find that you can do so much more. You will have capabilities unheard of for mankind, and although you may not have faith in yourselves at present in all your capabilities, even now you can do much more than you can possibly imagine. If you have faith in yourself and the God within you, you can do all things; as I said in My incarnation as Jesus, 'you can do all things through Christ'. You are never alone, God is always with you and within you, and so never be afraid, never be fearful that evil will overcome you because you are protected if you fill yourself with His Light and encircle yourself with the cloak of light, then no harm can befall you.

These are bewildering times for many of you because so many have been told of these changes, and you feel that so many versions are being written about it that you are not certain which one to believe. Each book that you read may differ slightly in facts, but there are always elements of truth given through those who channel Our words. Each one is attempting to bring through the truth although there are slight variations shall we say. It is not the fault of those who channel nor is it Ours, it is only that it is coloured by the personality of those bringing through Our communication. Just remember this and accept everything in this way. Reject what you cannot accept, but know that the truth is always being given, that the Earth and those upon it are changing and moving upwards to the fifth dimension slowly but surely.

Everything depends on the state of man at that time and should there be violence erupting everywhere, then the change will have to be more absolute, so the Earth will move on her axis if necessary. We hope that this will not be necessary and that the change will be less extreme, and that the thoughts and actions of men will have tempered to be less violent and more peaceful on the whole. Humanity is such that peace will never prevail constantly throughout the world. This would be miraculous if it happened, but miracles can happen, and We hope that We can accomplish much during these next few years to bring about changes in the thoughts of man, so that countries will be less divided and come together as one. Rather like the beings on Arcturus who all work together and try to serve one another, serving all for the benefit of the whole of the planet. They too had their time of change, but being on the fifth dimension now, they are great beings of light, and I know that they too are trying to help mankind through this transition. All of us are working together as one, the Master, those beings on other planets and the Angelic Hierarchy, all are serving God and trying to bring about the change as smoothly as possible. There are other planets like the Earth who will also be moving upwards, almost at the same time as yourselves, so that the whole movement will be Cosmic and all of you will come together onto the fifth dimension.

All of you will be able to attune to the Cosmic Consciousness more readily as time goes by, and this will be wonderful for you. You will find that you can know many things that are within you. Everything is within each one of you, all wisdom, but you cannot tap into this unless you have reached a level of consciousness that is higher than you have attained at present. In time, humanity will be wise beyond all conception, and this is what we are attempting to bring about a complete awakening to the Universal Mind, which is true reality. You may think that your physical life upon the Earth is the only thing that is real, but believe Me, many inhabitants of the Earth have much to learn in this respect. Many are completely unaware that there is such a thing as a Universal Mind, and that they have a spirituality of their own. They do not know that they are beings of light and in time to come, they will have to be awakened to this. If they cannot conceive of this reality, unfortunately they will have to be swept aside and reincarnate on another planet until they are ready to learn so much more about themselves, and raise themselves to a higher level of consciousness.

All of you on the spiritual path have been learning so much within the last decade, and you will recognise the fact that never has there been such an awakening in the history of man as now. You have chosen to incarnate at this time; it is a time of great happenings, it is a time for exhilaration for those who are becoming aware and raising their consciousness. Each one of you is learning as each day goes by, as the energies that are being poured into the Earth's atmosphere are being utilised by all of you to raise your consciousness. As a result, all of you are capable of attuning to higher beings more readily, and as each week, month and year goes by, this capability will become much stronger. You will recognise this when you sit in meditation, and become conscious that your guide or higher self is closer to you, and be in contact with them much quicker and easier than before. Accept this and know that it is part of Our work at this time, and realise that it is part of the proceedings in the Earth's changes.

You will find as time goes by that you will need less food. This will take time, but your lives will become less involved, and you will have more time to just BE, and to recognise the fact that this is part of your life; an important part, which must not be neglected, being at one with God. Looking within and hearing that still small voice, which is becoming louder. He wishes mankind to link with Him and be one with Him at this time. Even those of you who have very busy lives should make time for this quiet interlude each day. It is all part of His Plan for man's future, and as you become aware how this Plan is evolving, you will realise how important you are in God's Plan, and you will take part in this by helping others to understand, and they will more readily accept as the months go by. More are becoming awakened and will be ready to accept your words, and ready to accept that they are spirit in a living body. Always remember that you can accomplish so much more if you will have faith in our ways, and recognise those ways as being part of the Plan.

God bless and keep you always, Sananda.

TEACHINGS FROM THE MASTERS-3

Yes, it is Sananda here to greet you this day. My love surrounds you and all who live within the world at this time. Our energies of love are pouring forth to attempt to evoke that same love and understanding in the hearts of all men. It seems that this is successful, and more and more are beginning to see the light, and that light within is shining forth strongly to others. We find that through meditation, increasingly more people are reaching a higher level of consciousness, and this is what we wish to happen for all men. Throughout the world now as you know, there is a violent element, but we are attempting through our unconditional love, to gradually wipe away all that is evil and bring forth in mankind an understanding of one another, so that all become more compassionate and come together in thought, word and deed. We are working, as I have said before, with those beings who have helped mankind over the centuries, who come from other planets and with the Angelic Hierarchy. Together we hope that before the changes of the Earth become more apparent, that mankind will generate love to one another and prevent any more warring elements occurring.

Over the years since the Harmonic Convergence in 1987, there has been a channel opening up between the higher intelligences and those who are spiritually aware upon the Earth, and gradually, We feel that the energies that are pouring into the Earth are taking effect. There are more people who are becoming aware of their spirituality, and they are attempting to spread the word to others. This always takes time, and one has to choose one's moment to approach this subject with those friends and acquaintances who are not on that level, or you are not aware of their being on the spiritual path, and we hope that this element will gradually be more easily spread. The element of truth and the reality of the spirituality of man. Sometimes it can be given on a different level, even if you do not speak about it, you can lend a book which may touch on that subject, and this is useful for opening up the minds and hearts of those who have not yet come to this way of thinking.

It is difficult to broach this subject because it is perhaps nebulous to others, although they may go to church regularly and do good as far as they can, they may not have opened their minds to their capabilities of looking for and listening to that voice which comes from within. The voice of God or other beings who serve Him. They must be told that a prayer would be said before they meditate, to protect themselves from other beings who might impinge on their consciousness, and also before they leave their place of meditation. They should close down the chakras and surround themselves with light. All this you know, but it is just something that can be mentioned once they show any interest. Man's awakening is truly beginning, and we feel that more people are ready to accept the truth and spread this word, so that it has a snowball effect on all mankind. We hope that this will be so and that man's soul will evolve much faster than it has before.

There is so much to learn, and sometimes very little time in which to do so, so it is important that this word goes forth as well as any thoughts you yourself may have on the subject of man's spirituality. We are happy for you to spread your thoughts on this, which may be closer to reality because We Ourselves are beings of light who have been working on this for so long, that perhaps you are closer to those who have not yet seen the light. Always remember that you are beings of light also, much larger than you could imagine. Your light spreads upwards and around, and merges with those with whom you sit or walk, so that if a group of you are walking together, We look down and see you as one great mass of light spreading around far further than you can imagine. I have said before, that the light from Avatars and very evolved humanity is far greater than you could possibly conceive. The light from Sai Baba and Mother Meera is extensive, stretching right across the horizon for miles around.

We have the capability of seeing into the hearts of men and we know that mankind can be much greater than he is. He can do many things, which I as Jesus performed whilst incarnating; miracles, which at that time were deemed necessary to persuade mankind that God was working through Me, that He was, but needed that proof. You too, if you had the faith, can do what I did and more. I have said this previously, but it is so important that I sometimes repeat Myself on certain subjects to try to impinge these truths upon you and make you realise that it is possible for man if he is on the spiritual path and has great faith, that he too can perform some of the miracles that I did.

Sanat Kumara the Lord of the World, under whom I work, with the other Kumaras, commands Me to serve Him and to serve humanity through God's grace, and he wishes mankind to become one with Him; to become great beings who can serve God more powerfully as time goes by. Each being of light can merge in time to come with all others who are serving God, so that you become stronger and more powerful, to spread His goodness throughout the world. We have great expectations of what man will do, and there is a Plan for mankind, which We will guide you through when the time comes for this to take place. It involves many mysteries which are still to be unfolded upon the Earth, and at that time there will be a great surge of energies exploding from those key points throughout the world, which have power ready to be used and utilised for the good of the Earth and for mankind. That time is yet to come, and those who will be used at that time will be told, and the future of man looks great. He is heading for a unity, which has never been known for centuries; millennia, shall we say. It is necessary though for a clearance of violence, evil and negativity before that time arises. There will be a cleansing and purification of the Earth, and from that the phoenix will arise from the ashes; a new beginning and new Earth will come to pass, and from that great happenings will occur.

We hope that you will be a part of this, and that all will receive great benefits when that time comes. We know that light will spread from one horizon to the other, and that light of love and goodness will prevail, so the darkness will be swept aside, and all men will become one. You are heading for a new dimension, gradually your bodies are becoming adjusted, and through the new energies that are becoming new beings. At present you do not appreciate this, but in years to come you will appreciate that the changes have been occurring gradually to the Earth herself and to the atmosphere surrounding the Earth. Everything is beginning to change and when that full change occurs, the Earth will be a new Earth, newly risen from the ashes of the old, so that pollution will be a thing of the past, and mankind will rise into his own, becoming one with God. We are working on this, and all will be well. You do not need to fear anything as these changes come to pass. We will guide you and support you, and bring you towards this new Plan, which will take place in time to come.
May God bless you all and keep you in His care.
Sananda.

TEACHINGS FROM THE MASTERS-4

Peace be with you my child. I wish to speak about life on Earth; it is a time when experiences can be learned. It is a time of offering to God, offering your lives in service to Him and in love to one another. It is not easy to live upon the Earth. Life was not meant to be easy; it is a place of learning and through life's experience the soul evolves. When I was on the Earth as Jesus, I did not have an extremely easy life; it was one, which I felt was to be of service and which I enjoyed even though My life was a simple one. I did not have a home of My own and My disciples were My friends and My family for most of the life in which I served as Christ, but that matters not.

I experienced so much in those few years that I felt that My life was one in which I was a part of everything. Everyone, every being upon the Earth I was close to; the birds, animals, and the whole of nature was mine to experience because I was close to it, and in living close to nature one can learn how to cope better than those who are, shall we say, 'civilised' and living in a life of splendour, perhaps in a grand mansion or a palace far away from the realities of nature and life's experience. One can be too pampered, too estranged from the realities that the experience of life is not revealed in its entirety. As a result, the life lived in the lap of luxury is one which cannot be of great experience because there is no hardship. It is through hardship and perhaps pain that the experiences of life can be learnt, and the soul evolves faster in that way.

My wish for mankind is for him to experience everything that is possible in order to learn life's hard realities, although I do not wish for mankind to suffer unduly, but I do hope that your souls will evolve in this lifetime as quickly as they can, because this time of incarnating is a most important one for man. There is a quickening of energies pouring down upon the Earth, so that We who are guiding mankind can help him through this time of turmoil. But it is a time which will lead through to a wonderful new life where there will be no particular hardship, because there will be a new Earth and a new Heaven, which was foretold. The transition will be difficult briefly, but once you enter into this New Age, then there will be so much learnt, and you too will be a part of the whole of God's Creation and co-creators with God, experiencing new situations which have never been experienced on this Earth before. This new life will be one in which you will be able to stand back and take part in the whole of Creation. Perhaps it is something, which you have not thought too deeply about.

You will be able to raise your consciousness higher and be in tune with the Cosmos. You will be capable of linking with many beings of light who are unknown to you at present, and only those who can channel our thoughts can have some awareness that there are beings; great beings of light who are co-ordinating life here on Earth and on many other planets. It is part of the grand pattern, God's Plan for all Creation. Those beings of light may not be seen, or heard by others. Some may be able to occasionally see a wonderful light or a quick glimpse of something as though a veil has been lifted and a vision revealed of a being or several beings attempting to communicate, but that brief glimpse is only fleeting, whereas in the future you will all be capable of being in communication with and seeing the Masters of the Hierarchy and the Angelic Hierarchy, and all who are at present a part of the great Plan for the Cosmos will be revealed from time to time.

Once you have reached that higher dimension, there will be a new life for you which will be much simpler, and you will find less hardship because once you are free of the three dimensional life, it will be a completely different outlook for everything, and those who presently have much to do physically will find that their lives will be transformed. All of you will have a new existence, but there is a need still to love and help each another, particularly at the time of the transition. I know that those of you who are treading the spiritual path wish to be of service in your lives at present, both to God and to others. This is part of life's pattern, and service is the ideal way of being in balance with God, man and nature. Trying to keep from hurting or harming anyone, trying to be selfless and attempting to help others less fortunate than oneself, for all this is part of service and part of God's plan is for mankind to have this outlook. There are many who do not think in this way, but I am not speaking to them, I am at present speaking to those who wish to serve in any way they can.

Part of life's plan is to exist upon the Earth and bring about a new outlook, a loving outlook for one another, and to spread God's word and His light to those places upon the Earth which are in darkness, and where there is violence and evil around. God's light will over-come this, and if you can think daily of sending light to those dark places, then it will be overcome far faster than it would if all of you did not make a concerted effort to dispel it. Within each one of you there is light, God's Light that you can allow to flow freely from you to wherever you wish it to go, either to heal or to bring light to bear. It is a great power which man often is completely unaware of, but those who are aware of their spark of divinity can tap this source of light and power to send forth that which is needed. I hope that all of you will continue to amass more light as time goes by. All of you are lighted beings, and as you become more spiritually aware, that light glows stronger within you and around you, and you are capable of sending that power of light wherever you wish.

Utilise this and always think positive thoughts, and avoid negativity wherever you can. There is so much negativity in the world already, even your television programmes have to be chosen carefully. If you find there is too much violence and negativity, switch off and think positive loving thoughts to overcome the negativity that may have polluted you. It is important to think good thoughts because thought is so powerful that even an occasional dark thought which creeps in can have power, so be careful in whatever you say, do or think, because thoughts are living things. If you imagine the Akashic record upon which mankind's life is played out over the centuries past, that Akashic record is there, still around the Earth and we can see the darkness, evil and pain recorded on it forever. We know how much suffering there was in past wars because it is there shining darkly upon the ether, and we hope that once you have reached that new dimension, that this will be wiped out, and love, light and God's power will be recorded on it constantly, and joy will be man's future.

We know mankind wishes to improve, and know that through these thoughts and yearnings it will happen. If you truly wish it, then it will happen. As you know, prayer is most important in your life, and if it comes from the heart there is great power in it, so try to think clearly when you pray. Do not say the same prayer constantly without thought. Think clearly and enunciate your heartfelt wishes for the needs of others, and then those prayers will be answered. It may not be necessarily how you would wish, but in time those needs will be fulfilled and the wishes granted. Try to expect the best of everything for all your loved ones, and think positively that they will receive everything they need, and very often this will be fulfilled if it is God's will. Always think if God wills it; then let it be so. He has the last word but He wishes man to be happy, peaceful and love one another. This is the most important thing in life; sending out unconditional love to all who you come in contact with. If this is done throughout the world, then life on Earth will become a place where man can live in peace and harmony, and God will grant peace, and goodness will prevail.

The archangel Michael is working with the Hosts of Heaven at this time to bring about that peace, but He needs your help in this. Think of the invocation given by the Master R for the invocation of light. I will repeat it once again because it is an important invocation to know.

'Wielder of the sword come forth.
Defend man from his darkness.
May God's pure divine light shine through the hearts of men,
And love and peace prevail.'

Remember this and use it daily and the Archangel Michael will have more power to defend against the world's darkness with light. My love and blessings be upon you all this day.
God bless, Sananda.

TEACHINGS FROM THE MASTERS-5

My greetings to you this day, this is Sananda, and I wish to speak to you on health and healing. It is most important that the body is cared for as much as possible through diet and exercise if possible. Diet, as you are aware these days, is important for the welfare of the body. Natural foods are the best; everything that is grown upon the Earth, vegetables, nuts, fruits, seeds and pulses can be used. All these foods, either fresh or dried are the best in order to have the body in as perfect condition as can be maintained. Heavy foods are clogging and do not allow you to raise your consciousness higher, and heavy meals are not good because they prevent the mind from working easily. As you know, the mind, body and soul are all one, and it is important that the soul is housed in a temple fit for it. The body being the temple for the soul, it is man's responsibility to care for the body and keep it in good working condition in order that the soul may improve in each lifetime. That is the reason for living, to evolve the soul and provide it with unique experiences each time, life after life.

This life is one that is of vital importance. At the present time the Hierarchy is working with other beings of light from planets far more evolved than the Earth and other three-dimensional planets. They have great experience of life, not necessarily in the same way as you have, and they wish to help mankind at this time, and they are combining with us, the Masters and other beings of light such as the Archangels, Michael in particular. We are helping to provide man with energies that will raise his thoughts and consciousness to a new level of being. In these higher levels of awareness, once man has realised his potential, there is infinite possibility for experiencing new thoughts and learning the true realities of life.

Once man has realised that he is capable of many things, you will find that there will be a new race of men, which will develop and you are part of this new beginning. Those of you on the spiritual path are aware that through thought, you can do many things using this in a positive way rather than a negative way.

This new ideal has been developing gradually and we have been attempting to help you to create new ideas. It is always difficult to leave familiar things behind and to learn that change is necessary, but unless you change you cannot learn, you cannot create a new state of being unless you let go and move on with that flow of new ideas and new beginnings. Think of a small insect like a caterpillar, which constantly changes and develops new ways of living. It gradually turns into a chrysalis and during that time it changes and moves into a new beginning. Once it emerges from that chrysalis, it expands its wings and takes off into a new life. That small creature is emerging into a new state, and this is what we hope for mankind, that he will expand his awareness and know that through meditation and prayer he can reach up to new heights of being, linking with the higher realms daily. Allow that time, morning and night, for your link with God, and you will soon find that the link will be quicker as time goes by, becoming a simple matter, so that the link is constant and thoughts can be given to you from the higher realms as simply as breathing.

All of you will find that your capabilities will improve, and mankind will move into a new awareness, and lift into the fifth dimension. This transition stage between now and then is the time that we are concentrating on, to help man to adjust to these new ways of living and being, learning the true realities and tapping into that inner core which is filled with wisdom, and which can be used to the full in future days. Each one of you has this inner core of knowing, and it is only through meditation that this can be explored. Each one of you can do much more than you could ever imagine through this link and through your new way of thinking, using positive thought to the full, either for your own use in meditation or in healing. Sending forth this positive healing thought towards others whom you wish to help, and although you yourselves are not providing the healing, it is through your positive link with God and other beings of light that you can send forth this power.

Each one of you has this capability and once your link has become established and is constant, then you can always be capable of sending forth healing light towards any who require it, either near or far, it matters not. If you link in love, you can send this light across the world, distance is no object if you send it with love and compassion, then this power is ready to be tapped by anyone.

Your life on Earth is important. Remember that in each lifetime you are attempting to improve your soul, and some people are not aware that there is more than one life. You can help them by attempting to prove that they reincarnate, and though they may have had other lifetimes, this is the one that is most important because it is the one in which man can become a superbeing as you might say, one who is constantly in touch with the powers above. To be one who is between two worlds, the higher realms and life on Earth, but always remember that your life on Earth is not purely physical or material, but is spiritual as well. Although it is good to have time for leisure and enjoyment, that is only a part of your life, and it remains your responsibility to decide whether you wish to spend your life in leisure and enjoyment constantly, or if you wish to use your life to the full, both physically and spiritually, extending your capabilities so that you can link spiritually both with God and with other beings.

These beings from other worlds are here to help at this time, and if you are not aware of them, this matters not, but those who can link with them through thought can learn much and pass it on to others who will be ready to receive these thoughts. I know that you must have an open mind in order to actually believe that beings from other planets can contact humanity. These are many books on these subjects, and some of these have been channelled by sensitives who can receive this communication, and those who are interested can learn much if they have an open mind. Try to pass on as much as you can to others and help to unlock their minds, giving them new thoughts, by sowing a seed here and there so they too can absorb so much more than if their minds remained closed. They will learn a new reality and new ideas, so that they too will change and be ready to move on like the caterpillar into the butterfly.

All of you have the capability of progressing and realising your potential, and becoming that being of light that you truly are, much larger than you could imagine, and be capable of many things. When you move to the fifth dimension and become aware of much more than at present, you will meet many beings face to face in that dimension instead of through thought, and when this occurs your life will change and become more vital. Everything will change at that time, but this process has already begun, and this is why I spoke about diet and health because it is important that mankind changes his ways from now on. Many have already altered their diets radically over the last few years, and more are becoming aware that meat is not good for mankind.

The treatment of food nowadays has altered over the years, and as a result, foods that man had eaten in the past are not suitable now. Vegetarianism is ideal because all the foods eaten are natural and cannot harm man. Think on this because your bodies must change before you move onto this new level of being. The molecular structure will alter slowly but surely, so that the change is not too extreme, and you will find that your bodies will react less strongly if you are eating lighter foods, those foods which I as Jesus and my disciples ate when we moved about from place to place. We ate simple natural fruits and we carried the basic food with us wherever we went.

It is this thought that I put into your minds, to try to live in a simpler way, less complex foods in your diet, so that your link with the higher realms becomes easier, so that your meals do not weigh you down, and your link with God becomes more powerful as time goes by. We will guide you to this new way of living, and the wonderful change that will come about as you move from the old to the new. Go with the flow of all the energies, which are being poured into the Earth, and will help you to change your way of life to a better way, a new way, which we will gradually help you to experience. So much to look forward to, and we wish you well.

God bless and keep you all, Sananda.

TEACHINGS FROM THE MASTERS-6

Yes it is Sananda who speaks to you this day. I wish you all well, and I do hope that My talk today will be of interest to you. It is about light and colour. Light is essential to all life, as you know it. You could not live and be supported without the light of the Sun; its power upon the Earth is all-important to everything that dwells upon the Earth. When you look back in the history of mankind when there was no lighting in houses, everyone was dependent upon the Sun for light to work and live by. Therefore, particularly in time of winter when the days were very short, everything had to be done much quicker. There was little time to spend on making things to support them in the winter, so the time of great activity was during the summer time when days were longer. Eventually man was able to make artificial light for himself and could then employ the long winter evenings working by man-made light. Though, think of the growth of plants and fruits, everything that grows upon the Earth needs light. All beings on all planets need light, and therefore when you think of life, you think of light, because all beings have within them that light which is God, and it is so, even if many are completely unaware of it.

Therefore, light is everywhere and even in the darkness there is light, because there is the light of God within you, and when you think of white light, the colours of the spectrum when split up are within that white light. It contains a rainbow of colours as you know, and you have all seen light shining through glass from time to time with a rainbow effect reflected within the room, and children delight in seeing this, as well as looking at oil lying on water, with sunlight shining upon it, showing those rainbow colours. This colour which is contained within the light is most important, for colour plays an important part within the life of man, even though he is rather unaware of this. When you visit the countryside and see the beautiful green of grass and leaves surrounding you, it is so harmonious you cannot conceive of nature's colours clashing with each other, they never do, they always blend beautifully and that blending of colour within the life of man is an important integral part of living. You could not imagine living with a room painted brilliant red; it would be most disturbing to the soul. It is always a subtler colour that is used for house paint, and every colour is chosen carefully by those who use it for a room in which they live.

In hospitals particularly, it is important to use colours, which are soothing; greens and pale yellows that are uplifting and soothing, in order that healing may take place. When colour is used in healing it is used by those who know alternative means of healing. It is not normally used by general medical doctors, but even in traditional medicine it is generally known that certain colours are unsuitable for healing. Certain therapists use colour to heal the soul and body, and green and blue are used to give soothing energy and give support to those who need to be calmed, and allay tension and stress. For boosting energy the red colours are used, to give positive thoughts, and give support to those who need to be energised, and therefore the warm colours are ideal for this, red, orange and yellow, which are filled with life-giving forces. There is much known about colour now which was not known in the past, and those who are aware of colour being important, know instinctively what is right at certain times for people who come to them for help.

Light is life and within all beings that light within is the life-giving force from God. Those in spirit are filled with light, and that world of spirit, which impinges upon the world of men, is the world of light, which you have come from, and to which you will return. Think of that world of light, which is rather like a parallel world to the Earth. You know that we in the world of light that surrounds you are here, and we can see you even though you cannot see us. Some are gifted as clairvoyants and can see at certain times, seeing auras surrounding those who are upon the material plane. They can see the shining light surrounding people who stand in front of them, and they can also see beings of light at certain times, but mostly humanity knows that there is a world of light to which they will return, and to know is to be aware, so this awareness is important, and is an integral part of living. If you are unaware and do not believe in that world of light to which you will return, it is very sad. Some people think that this physical life they are presently living is the only life there is, and that when they die that is the end of them. They do not realise they are filled with light, and their soul, that light, will return home. They do not realise that there is a life hereafter, and they presume that when the spirit leaves them, the shell or body is buried, and that is the end of their life entirely.

These people do not have the power of awareness, and do not know that life continues everlastingly, and that they themselves have lived before. Perhaps they are new souls who have not been able to learn the truth of life, and how important that light within them is, and it links with all other lights surrounding them. The lights within each one of you, that light of God, and He is everywhere of course because He links all of you together, so that there is no separation. Those who have gone before you are linked to you in this way, and those who will come who await incarnation, are also linked with light, so that truly light pervades everything throughout this physical world of the Earth. The realm of light which surrounds it, and those planets which are within reach of the Earth, many of which have other beings of light upon them, living in different forms; they too are a part of everything and everyone. When you think of your past, you may presume that you have always lived upon Earth in past lives, but this is not necessarily so, for you may have originated from another planet in the past and have lived with other beings on that planet, who are not necessarily of human form, possibly similar but not the same.

Though all are filled with that light which is God, and therefore it makes you realise how immense and all-powerful that light is.

The Source of all being is that great powerful God who is omnipresent; and you are aware that I am one of the Kumaras, and serving God by working constantly to bring as much light of knowledge and power to humanity so that all can benefit from this light of wisdom. There is much to be done within the next few years to raise the consciousness of mankind so that he becomes a truly lighted being. You are aware that meditation and a linking with your higher self are all-important. You know that your inner life, although less obvious than the normal outer self of your physical being is nonetheless most important, so try to integrate your inner being with your outer being and concentrate on improving your capabilities of linking with the realms of light. This is part of your evolvement, all are reaching towards the light and in doing so, you will learn many truths from within. Everything that is known which is important can be taped from your inner self; therefore all wisdom can be yours if you can learn how to tap this source of knowledge.

Many there are who can link easily with this Source, who have done little reading of learned books. If they can tap into this all-powerful ageless wisdom they do not need to use books, they can just learn from within, and we hope that they will pass on this wisdom that they have to others who have not yet learnt how to find this key to knowledge. All of you have this capability, and if you will just learn to turn within and seek, you will find all you need to know. Therefore, remember that it is this link with the light within, which pervades everything; this is the key to your learning in this lifetime. Pass on this knowledge and try to extend the capabilities of all with whom you come in contact. All who will accept their capabilities. It is not everyone to whom you can turn and give this knowledge to, I am aware of this, but try to extend your capabilities and those with whom you can talk on this subject, and in time mankind will learn to use light to the utmost, using light so that it is transformed into knowledge. Remember this, that light is most important and can be utilised in so many ways.
God bless and keep you all, Sananda.

TEACHINGS FROM THE MASTERS-7

This is Master R, and I greet all who read these words with love and peace. This is what we hope for mankind in future days, that violence will be overcome, and love and peace prevail; this was part of the Invocation that I gave in my last communication in Book 1. Michael, the Wielder of the Sword of Light will continue to help mankind at this time. He is serving God and us, the Masters, and he is working against the forces of evil. At this time in man's history we recognise this as a great force, because although there have always been wars since very early on in man's past, at this time it is certain men of power who are attempting to fight the will of God. They have no time for goodness and purity, they are the forces of darkness and it is this power that we fight, the power of evil. We do not fight as such, we just send forth light to encompass the darkness, and in that light pure love dwells. Remember always that your light within is God, and that God is pure goodness, so that if you attempt always to serve Him and extend your light outwards towards others, then God will prevail and others always recognise light, love and joy within you. They will be drawn to you because those who are encompassed in light repel negativity and darkness.

We, from the realms of light have been watching mankind over the centuries, and at this time in the history of man, it is good to be alive. So many wish to help at present and are waiting in the sidelines, so to speak, to incarnate at this time. It is a time of great import and much will be achieved if you and others of like mind will extend your consciousness, raising and reaching ever upwards to pure light. I have been telling the one who is channelling this communication that if you do this reaching upwards, visualising magenta, you will find it easier to communicate with those from the light realms. It is very pure and it is nearest to our vibratory level. The nearest that man can achieve, so that if you can reach this level each time you meditate, it will be beneficial, because you will find it much simpler to receive any communication given to you. It may be that you will not be aware of words, but you may be given symbols and other colours which may mean something if you can decipher it, but in time if you persevere, you will receive words from those who wish to speak to you, beings of light, your guide or your higher self. Just be still and listen to that still small voice within you. You will be surprised at what you can achieve if you take time to reach up to this colour in each meditation.

It matters not if you cannot do this, but from time to time it will be helpful if you can spend longer to try to link with this colour. Colours of gold or greenish-blue are very powerful also, and if you can reach upto these levels, you will find that you can listen to communications, which normally you would not find very easy.

Each one of you may find that a certain colour is suitable for you alone, and whatever is best for you, attempt to achieve that colour in your meditation. I know that all of you are aware that meditation is all-important in your life, even if you only spend a short time morning and evening to link with those in the realms of light; that is sufficient. Many of you have busy lives and I know time is important but do spare a few minutes at these times and you will find it of great benefit. You will achieve much within your life, accepting that your spiritual nature is as important as your physical nature. Once you have walked the path of spirituality, you do not deviate from it because you have discovered a new dimension. You have reached what is necessary in your life, part of your life's destiny, and although you may not know what you chose to do in this lifetime, at least you have gone part of the way towards that goal by walking this road which may not be easy.

Life was not meant to be easy, and once you have accepted that fact, then part of life's troubles will be over, because the acceptance of this reality is important. You will then know and continue with your life as you would wish to. Wisdom can then be given to you, and that what you chose to do is being achieved slowly but surely. It is only given to a very few to know what you chose when you came into this incarnation. Those who are Avatars or Masters are aware from an early age, but most of you stumble through life and try to do your best, and having achieved a spiritual awareness, you will then link and achieve beneficial communications, which will give you a knowledge of the Ancient Wisdom as time goes by. This has been given to man over many centuries, and is a part of his inheritance, but you cannot achieve it unless you seek and knock on doors, which will be opened gradually as you reach higher levels of wisdom. Do not ever turn back and feel you haven't achieved anything. Keep on knocking and seeking for more wisdom and it will truly be given to you in due course.

Civilisations have come and gone over the millennia since man first came to the Earth. There have been those who have had great knowledge in the past, which has been lost to mankind. There have been the Egyptians, the Mayan, the Incas and the Aztec civilisations; all who had great knowledge. Some has been left for those who can read the hieroglyphs of tablets in those remote areas, and even long before that, there were the Lemurians and Atlanteans. All these known civilisations have learnt that within them there is the knowledge that can be given directly from God, so these truths although lost to man, can be regained if you learn to tap the source of all knowledge, which is within each one of you. All these civilisations including the ancient Greek culture knew these truths, and they left it above doorways, "Man know thyself, and thou shalt know the Universe", was one, and is still intact over certain doorways in parts of Greece and Italy. It has been known for many centuries, so nothing is truly lost. You have within you great power; learn how to tap this, and you and others like you will regain the wisdom of the ages.

We know that man having put his foot upon the path of knowledge; wisdom and spirituality will never turn aside. He will continue onwards, searching for all the truths that are within. Be as those in the past, filled with this great knowledge, and you will be a new culture of light, man as he truly is; a being of light made in the image of God. Know that the future of mankind is one, which will be great. You yourselves know that darkness will be prevailed upon by the light, which will shine forth from you all. Know that God is within each one of you and God will prevail. You can do all things through faith in Him. I give you my blessings this day and wish you well. Go in faith and love. God bless, Master Rakoczi.

TEACHINGS FROM THE MASTERS-8

My greetings to you this day, it is Master R. This is a propitious day to receive my words. The alignment of the planets and the full moon are important at certain times, and this is one of those times when the alignment is right. I know that there will be many thousands in this country and throughout the world working today for the improvement of the consciousness of man, and for the energising of the Earth's structure. There will be a great improvement both in the consciousness of mankind and the upliftment of the vibrations of the Earth after today's work. So many have come together in thought, and others meeting together now physically to bring about this change through the sounding of the OM. It will cause many things to occur today which might not have happened for many years. It is good that mankind has recognised this fact and has spread the word, because it may be that through this sound projection there will be less pain caused, less catastrophe of any kind when the transition comes about into the fifth dimension.

As you know there have been subtle changes occurring over the past few years, and they will continue so that mankind will gradually find his way into a new realm, a new dimension, and as this is happening, the Earth too is raising to a higher level. All these changes have been coming about gradually, but today will see the beginning of a new change in the history of mankind. This sounding of the OM together is the first time that man has actually attempted to uplift the energies and remove much of the negativity that has been caused recently. It has built up and this meeting together of those on the spiritual path will bring about a unique change in linking the two realms, and thinning the veil between the spiritual and physical realms. I know that you are part of that band of people, including all who read this, that within your hearts all you wish for is for negativity to decrease and an upliftment in the hearts and minds of mankind.

We, within the Hierarchy of the Masters and the Angelic Hierarchy have been working towards this end for a long time, and we are extremely pleased to see that our efforts have not been in vain. We know that there have been many unseen workers who have served us in this, including the many guides and other beings of light who have brought about this change. We feel that through this coming together of many of mankind's spiritual brotherhood, there will be a complete and utter change in the hearts of men. It is an historical day, and we hope that from now on, there will be an upsurge in the upliftment of man's vibratory level. It may not be anything dramatic to begin with, it may not be apparent for some time, but you will see changes taking place throughout the world, and gradually the Earth herself will rise into the fifth dimension. We have been telling you that all this will come to pass within five years and we feel more strongly that it will. As you know time is man made, it does not exist apart from on the Earth, and therefore you are aware that time is difficult for all of us to judge.

So much is also dependent upon man's free will and you cannot generalise in this because there are so many who think differently to yourselves, that everything is rather nebulous in terms of time. Everything depends on the majority of mankind turning aside from negativity and violence and changing their ways to that of peace and goodwill, and a new way of thinking. In this I mean your lives will be altered in many ways so that the majority will be living with their consciousness permanently attuned to God so He can speak to you directly into your souls, as it was when man first roamed the Earth. As he was when man was more of a being of light, more amorphous and permanently capable of having God speak directly to him.

In this way, all of you will be as man was then and your lives will change dramatically. Life will be more of a pleasure, and you will be able to recognise that divinity within and be able to link with the presence of God whenever you need help of any kind. He will be there as He is now, but so often it takes some time to link with your mind to God for His help, especially at a time of great need. It means that when there is danger at any time, normally you get on your knees and pray, and then God will answer you in His own way, but in future times you will not need to consciously link in prayer, for your life will be a prayer.

At present, to be able to attune to the realms of light, you really need to be in an altered state of consciousness, so that your whole being is linked with us, your thoughts put aside and your only intent is to link with us. In the future this will be much simpler, and we will be able to guide you much more easily than you are guided at present. Inspiration will be given and much good will come of this, so that as you know, the inspiration of art, literature and music is given frequently to those who can link with us. But in future, this will be constant, so those who are capable of transmitting these inspirations to paper in the form of music, art or writing will find that great works will come about through this permanent linking with the realms of light. You will have wonderful music composed in future times, which will be truly divine.

You have been told in the past that when you look at one another you can see the God within looking at you from the eyes of the one you behold, and this is so. Many times it has been said that the eyes are the windows of the soul, and truly they are. Remember that the light within each one of you is a small part of God, and you are all one in His eyes. Many have told you that there is no separation, and that you are all one and this is also true. The truth must be repeated so often. I am sure that sometimes you feel that this repetition is perhaps rather boring, but unless we keep on mentioning these obvious points, it cannot be stressed too often that the truth is there, and so often the truth is so simple. I think that mankind perhaps thinks that the truth must be very intricate and involved, and unless something is described in a complex way, then it is not the truth, but believe me, truth must out, and everything that is given in these communications is the truth. There is a golden thread which links you with the spiritual realms, and it links you with one another, and it links with that spark of divinity within each one throughout the world. Whether they know it or not, each one has that within them, and it is upto them to discover it and attempt to make it a great flame of light, that spark within which can glow more strongly as time goes by if it is fanned into the consciousness of the soul involved.

I know that all of you have the capability of improving your vibratory level through meditation, and raising your consciousness consciously, attempting to reach up to that level that is of the magenta colour, which you know is the highest you can achieve. You know that you are beings of light, and you know that if you are aware of that divinity within, then nothing can harm you. Live in the light, despite your physical bodies, for you can be directly linked with God and truly work for Him in this life. He wishes you to work together to perform miracles now and in the future. In working together, as is occurring today, both at Wembley and centres throughout the world, miracles will happen and you will see that there will be many changes come about in the very near future. We have been working towards this end and we know that now is the beginning of that change in heart; the change which is going to occur from now onwards.

The power points throughout the world, which will be energised on this day, will bring about a tremendous change within the structure of the Earth. So many places will be affected that you cannot imagine how this will come about, but there are still many unseen places of power that man has yet to discover, and they too will come into operation through the work that is done this day. That upsurge of consciousness from noon today will bring about many changes in the Earth's structure through sounding the OM and bringing that vortex of power to fruition. We are looking forward to these changes, and we know that men of goodwill will continue with the work, which was begun today. We wish you all well and we know that through this upsurge of power, there will be a new beginning upon the Earth. All is well, the Plan is continuing and your purpose in life is coming to pass.

God bless and keep you all,

Master Rakoczi.

TEACHINGS FROM THE MASTERS-9

If you wish to live a life believing in your own spirituality, then you must be filled with self-belief. Filled with the knowledge that the 'I AM' presence is within you and within all sentient beings. You must believe in yourself and leave no room for doubt or else small doubts and negativity will creep into your consciousness, and this is not good. You are a being mainly of spirit, living in a physical body at this time in the here and now, and the capability is within you of voicing the thoughts of other beings of light as this communication demonstrates, but you must be filled with confidence before you can accomplish this. At times, mankind is filled with doubt and wonders whether he is capable of dealing with many things, even trivialities from time to time.

Some never have doubts, and they are filled with confidence and they are truly leaders of men, and they continue throughout their lives living each moment filled with positivity and the knowledge that they can accomplish anything they wish to. Mostly, these leaders of men have a faith in God, and faith in themselves, putting their lives in God's hands, and this is how all men should live their lives if it is at all possible, knowing that their faith will bring them through to accomplish whatever they wish.

This is how God wishes man to be, but certain leaders have no scruples or morals, and these are the ones who have put their trust in someone other than God. They have gone astray; for they are men who only wish for self power, and have just turned from the belief that God will guide them. They have discovered that they can accomplish more things through cruelty and their own evil power. Perhaps they began their lives believing in God, but they have now become gods in their own minds, and believe that they can do all things without God. Do not turn aside from Him. Allow Him into your lives and know that you can do everything you wish to do to help others, but this can only be accomplished through God's help.

Those despots are not attempting to help others to come through trials and tribulations, or to listen to them in times of trouble. They do not have any care for others, for they only wish to continue to gain more confidence, and become stronger and this strength has been achieved, not by helping others but by trampling through life attempting to become all powerful, causing distress, and particularly in times of war, death and destruction, all for power.

The power from God is a gentle power, but it is omnipotent, and it can help to alleviate pain, and overcome negativity and danger. You all know when you have faced distress of any kind, for when you turn to God; He can help you to overcome anything. If you pray to God, He will alleviate your distress, doubts and fears. You are never alone in this life if you know that He is with you at all times. He is that 'I AM' presence within you; allow that presence to help you whenever you feel any doubts rising within you. What is life without faith, love and hope? All this is yours, for you can have whatever you wish if you will only ask. When you come to a crossroads in your life do you concern yourselves with small details and keep wandering off the point, becoming bogged down by trivialities? Try to muster all your forces together, as an army is brought to command by a General. He will see that everything is brought to order, and will have a clear insight into what is going to occur; you should try to collect your thoughts and keep them orderly. Perhaps at a time like this you should always remember that you can ask and you will receive what is necessary. God will guide you through any doubts, and He will help you if you will bring Him into your lives.

At times you may think that your life is full of problems, but these problems are put there for a purpose. A life without problems would be rather superficial in which you would learn nothing. Life is for learning, and through experiencing these problems and coming to terms with them, you are rising above and learning through these problems. Some people may feel that they have more problems than others, but this is not usually so. It all evens out, and you will find that through your life there are many times when there is great happiness; you may not think so at the time until you reflect upon it, and realise that you have been fortunate compared with many. Think of the suffering that has happened in Rwanda and remember that you have never had to face problems on this scale. Always be thankful for what you have, and grateful for the pleasures that you have received. It is at times when you see this suffering on television that you realise how fortunate indeed you are to have the life that you are living, and that the problems are small compared with those who have suffered the violence in Rwanda, Bosnia and other places.

You sometimes wonder why people should have to suffer on such a large scale, especially the babies and children who have died, who have done nothing wrong. Everything seems to be against them, and sometimes these things occur, seemingly purposelessly, but they are receiving racial karma. As you know, each one of you has to face the law of cause and effect, karma, which is something that you repay or are given. You have to pay back something, which you have incurred either earlier in this lifetime, or from another lifetime, which is more usual. You may have caused suffering to someone in a past life, and you have to receive suffering now or in your future life, to pay back this debt, and these people are repaying a debt which they owed in a past life. It may be that they were part of Hitler's S.S. who caused great suffering during World War Two, or it may be from something even further back in history.

It may seem to you unfair that these people and their children who appear to have done no harm are suffering so much, but they have chosen to repay this. They have come into this life knowing that they will repay some powerful karma, which they owed. You may feel great sorrow for them and this is only natural because they have gone through so much, but realise that they have learnt through this and are continuing to learn in this lifetime, so try to accept this knowledge and recognise it for what it certainly is, karma; racial karma. You recognise this, and realise that from time to time this does happen, as it has in various other violent acts of war in recent years, but it is still sad that these people have had to suffer, and your hearts go out to them. You have been sending out light towards these areas for some time; those of you who are spiritually aware, and I know that this light has helped to send love and comfort to all at this time. Nothing is wasted, and if you send out light and love it always helps, and even though the suffering goes on, they can endure it more easily if they receive this light and love from others.

It is the same when healing is given to someone who is really extremely ill, and perhaps will pass into the spiritual realms very shortly. In other words they will 'die', which is the word more frequently used on Earth, but as you know nobody dies, they just pass into another dimension and leave their bodies behind, so when healing is given at this time, it is always helpful. God's healing light will give them comfort, and although you may feel that you have failed if giving them His healing, realise that they are being helped on another level. They will receive this power, and it will help them to cope with their illness. They recognise that healing is being given and will be uplifted through this healing light, even though they are not successfully cured. Healing is never wasted, and the intent is good for they recognise this and are grateful for your help at any time.

When healing is given to children it is so simple because they do not try to reject anything, they absorb it as do animals, and there is a very quick reaction through the healing light passing into them. They are healed very simply in a way adults aren't, as the healing light is absorbed into their bodies and souls without any barrier. They are such innocent creatures, children and animals, that the healing is not restricted in any way. I mean that some adults are rather wary about receiving healing and there is a slight barrier to the healing light, but mostly this healing light is accepted by all and gratefully received from those who are the intermediaries between God's healing Light and the patient.

Everything in life is made complex by men's minds, but everything is quite simple really if you will accept the fact that God can help all of you at any time. He is there to guide and comfort you at all times. We hope that you will always accept this and know that it is so. I, the Master R have been attempting to pass on knowledge to mankind for many centuries, and over this time I have used many channels to pass on this knowledge to all who have ears to hear. Please accept these thoughts and dwell on them in your hearts. Be still and have faith, and all will be well.

God bless and keep you all,
now and always, Master Rakoczi.

TEACHINGS FROM THE MASTERS-10

Man's life is a testing ground of experience, and there are so many tests to go through from childhood to the end of a lifetime. There is so much to learn, and as you go through your life and reflect on what has been experienced within it, you will find you have had many difficulties and experiences to deal with, such as hurt, pain, illness, insecurity, loneliness, danger; many things which have to be learnt. It is through these experiences that man learns to cope with triumph and disaster, and within your life you will find that through faith there will be help given to you from God.

Certain people have no faith or belief in the existence of God, and they travel through their lives depending purely upon themselves, thinking that at the end of that life, that is the end and there is nothing beyond it, and it is only at certain times when disaster strikes, that a change comes into their thought process, and they realise that they have been entirely wrong, and through this experience many of them return to God.

I say return, because probably in a past life they have turned aside from God, and although they knew that He existed, they have just lost their faith. Therefore in this lifetime they began in this way, and then rediscovered that God is always there to help, guide, comfort, and give healing if they will allow Him to do so. What is more, they have re-learnt that faith can move mountains. We know that man, through this learning process of experiencing hardship in many forms, will turn to God and recognise that it is all part and parcel of life, and that it is necessary to have faith in order to cope with the realities of life.

Sometimes even though you have a loving nature, others may hurt you and you must hold firm to your faith. Do not feel that a reprisal is necessary because it is not, and even though you have been spitefully used, you should just try to walk away from that situation. Turn the other cheek and recognise that God is within each one of you, and the person who has hurt you will be penalised in time to come, and that penalty will be given tenfold to make up for the hurt, the slight that has been given to you. Never feel that everything is against you and never feel that you should get your own back in any way. However hurt you have been, you must carry on and put it at the back of your mind. Do not dwell on these things, but be positive and loving towards all, even those who hate you.

It is all part of God's plan for humanity, that some people have this unfortunate attitude to others, and the love that is within them has been blocked in some way. Perhaps they have been hurt badly in the past and are retaliating in return. Try to understand this and then you will recognise this weakness within them. I know that at times it is difficult to turn the other cheek, but if you turn to God and pray to Him for help, you will find that the bitterness will go and warmth will flow into your heart once more. Never feel that coldness overcoming you; you must not allow this to happen. Try to recognise that all have that divinity within if they will allow it to flow from one to another, and in this way, men will truly form a brotherhood.

Some have more to learn than others, and although their lives seem very hard, those who have been disabled from birth or mentally affected in some way as children; they often are the most cheerful of beings. They appear to have an inner strength which 'normal people', shall we say do not have, but this inner strength is given to them from God, and they have a cheerfulness within them which cannot be dissipated. It is wonderful to see, and many lessons can be learnt from watching people who are affected in some way and yet are disaffected by it, and have the sunniest nature of all. Truly God is working through them and there is much to be learnt from this.

It is always recognised that mankind was made in the image of God, and as such he has a responsibility to face up to; to be as God would wish him to be in his dealings with others. Try to remember this always in your lives, acting out your lives as though you were part of Him. You know that you should live a life that is honest, loving and peaceful. Certain peoples upon the Earth find this very hard at present, where there is violence and suffering in certain areas throughout the world. It is difficult for those people to be loving and peaceful under those conditions, but as I said, life is a testing ground for all, and they are truly being put to the test at this time. It seems unfair you think, for all these innocent children to suffer, but they have chosen to incarnate in this situation, in order to learn through this suffering and to experience many unfortunate conditions.

Always there is a choice for mankind for evil or good. At present it seems as though there is much evil in the world, but if you look around, there is plenty of goodness as well, and many times the youth are blamed for violence and crime, and so many of them are completely innocent. It is only a small minority who are acting in this way and causing others to condemn the whole of their generation. Perhaps they have been brought up in a time when violence is accepted mainly through the media, and there is much to answer for in this way, because through violent television programmes, the young are brainwashed into thinking that this is normal, whereas it is completely abnormal. If you watch that type of film or programme it can have an effect upon you, a negative effect, the same as horror films and ghost films which are shown late at night. Try to avoid these at all costs because there is enough negativity in the world without dwelling upon such horrors.

Try to be positive in your thoughts and attitudes in life, and radiate this positivity and love towards all with whom you come into contact. Goodness will then prevail if more will accept this and not dwell upon negative programmes, and negativity in newspapers. It is as well to leave them alone, and just try to live out your lives in normal conditions. By all means keep up with the news as it happens, but do not dwell on sadness and negativity. Send out light to those areas where it is necessary. Light and love and healing will then prevail there, but never dwell upon sadness. By all means pray for these people because prayer is extremely powerful, as you know. Man has been praying through the millennia, and Western man has always felt that prayer was sufficient. It is always extremely good, and if it is done with powerful thoughts, hopes and desires, then God will take note, but meditation too is very powerful, as the Eastern religions have known through the centuries, but it is only of recent times that the Western civilisation has recognised the necessity to meditate, and to still the mind and allow God to come into your very being. He is always there, but be aware of Him and have that peaceful time each day with a stilled mind. It helps to relieve tension and brings healing and peace to the soul.

There is so much noise and bustle in life that a half hour or more each day can make such a difference to the life that is filled with activity. Obviously when you are incarnating, you must participate in physical work and meeting others, but there is always time for leisure as well, and this should be given to all. Work hard, play hard and pray hard; all these things are a part of life and each one is important in itself, so remember this. Allow time for all these things in your life each day, for it is important to have a balanced life, otherwise one part will overtake the other. It is important that you should have time to be still, and more than ever, as life is extremely busy for most of you, and it makes a difference if you can allow yourself time for a quiet peaceful meditation each day. I know it is very difficult for some of you to fit this in, but if you can, then you will find that your life is easier to cope with.

Remember always that man is capable of much more than he could ever imagine spiritually, and that his spirituality is most important. Life is both physical and spiritual, and if you can raise your consciousness within your lifetime to be one with God, then you will have achieved much. You recognise this from other lifetimes once you have achieved oneness, and it is through this realisation that you have been one with other beings of light in the past, and that you will find that as time goes by, it will become easier to achieve a higher level of consciousness, and that oneness will be an important part of your life. Be still and know that you are God.
Blessings be upon you all,
Master Rakoczi.

TEACHINGS FROM THE MASTERS-11

We from the higher realms continually watch over mankind and his works, hoping always that there will be improvements right across the board, both in the consciousness of man, and everything that he achieves. Much has been achieved over the last few decades in this respect, and we still hope that there will be an upliftment of consciousness so that violence that occurs in different parts of the world will gradually be depleted. There has been a change of thought in Ireland, and we hope this will be maintained, and also in the Middle East; that this too will be a peace that is lasting and true. Eventually we hope that sporadic fighting throughout the world will cease, and mankind will be a brotherhood in the truest sense.

We, the Masters are always striving to help and keep returning to the Earth to be one with man, because although we have achieved much over our lifetimes and mastered everything, we return from time to time and are part of humanity. We help in different ways to make man realise that he is capable of so much more than he could ever imagine, and to bring this to bear so that the fruition achieved in each lifetime is one that is truly great.

Speaking generally to all who read this; I am trying to make you realise that in your life you can achieve more than you would ever imagine possible if you will have true faith in your capabilities, and in the knowledge that you can do all things through Christ if you truly wish it. To raise the consciousness both of yourself and others who will listen to the words that you may give them. To offer words of encouragement and inspiration which have been given to you in your meditations, and perhaps through reading books, which have been inspired from higher realms, and from the Masters of the Hierarchy.

There are certain times in your life in which you may reflect. You can be enjoying activities and relationships with others with whom you have much in common, when suddenly one of you is struck down, either through illness or is incapacitated in some way, and there seems to be no reason for it, but sometimes this occurs to make that person stop doing and just BE. So that they are unable to travel or do very much apart from read, meditate and contemplate, and perhaps this is something that is necessary at this time. Perhaps that individual needs to reflect on his life, and raise his consciousness to a higher level, a higher capability of inspiration, and make contact with those in the higher realms who wish to help him achieve more spirituality, and therefore his physical life has been put on hold. This may occur perhaps to someone who has been leading a very active life until then, and it seems most unfair at the time, but on reflection it will be noted that it was necessary for that rest to take place and the opportunity given to just BE.

Healing will take place as a rule if that individual is healthy, and should usually become fit in a short while, but that opportunity has been given to allow the spiritual nature to develop alongside the physical, so the individual is more balanced and rounded, shall we say. It is so easy for the nature of man to be seen as purely physical, whereas the spiritual side can be neglected, and it is most important that it is given a chance to develop and mature, particularly if he is an old soul, who has been incarnating many, many times. It is easy to forget the spiritual nature, but once it has been awakened, then it cannot and shouldn't be allowed to be neglected, and it will grow, mature and evolve as it is meant to. Souls that have experienced many lifetimes are capable of absorbing many things within a short space of time, and the learning that has taken place in other incarnations comes to the fore in that individual, once it has been given the opportunity to just BE for a while in that life.

As you have been told many times, it is necessary to have that quiet time each day in meditation and prayer. I am sure that all of you remember this within your daily life, but it is sometimes neglected by certain individuals, and until they have this opportunity to just BE instead of rushing off to work each day and returning tired, this time of being incapacitated is invaluable to them. It has been given to them to experience that challenge to reach upwards and inwards to the God within who is waiting for that contact.

Life on Earth is very precious, and it is up to each individual to use it to the full. To recognise that they have the power within them to be in contact with God, their guides or other beings in the spirit world who are waiting, like ourselves the Masters, for that recognition that each one of you is truly spirit attempting to evolve during that life on Earth. So much more can be achieved in this way, and our inspiration can help to make that individual aware of so many things. Life is a training ground for all; and over these next few years the energies, which have been generated and expanded recently will be helping each one of you to achieve more in this lifetime than ever before.

Some of you may not be aware of this change, and this does not matter so long as you participate in meditation day by day, attempting to be inspired in that quiet time. There are many who are aware of this new energy, which abounds, and which is generating the Earth into a higher dimension slowly but surely, so all of you are gradually moving into that new higher dimension. Change is all around and even the animals are aware of this. They too are changing and adapting so they can live as one with you. There is gradually coming about an alteration in man's attitude towards the animals, though it is slow, but it is coming to pass that there are less people who consume meat. Even those who have always done this without a thought are recognising the fact that it is not necessary to eat meat as part of the diet. They are changing their ways, and recognise the fact that animals have just as much right to live on the Earth as mankind, and that man as custodian of the Earth and everything upon it has a great responsibility towards animals and all other life on Earth.

A new awareness is slowly coming about, and in time we feel that man will become truly as he was when he first evolved, eating only the fruits and seeds of the Earth, not killing to eat or for sport, but truly aware that all are one, and all are a part of God and His Creation. God's Plan is beginning to come about, and we the Masters trust that you and others of like mind will continue to spread His word, and continue to try to be better individuals. Awareness that you should attempt to be in His image, acting as He would wish you to, for you are inheritors of God's Plan on Earth, and be His representative to all. Each one of you truly has a great responsibility in each lifetime as His representative on Earth, to try to be, as He would wish. This is something that we have known, and have attempted to do whenever we return to Earth, to help His world and bring about His Plan.

I, the Master R am appointed to do this, and do it in remembrance of Master Jesus, who is now Sananda, and is doing this and other work, which is most exacting. All of us are a part of God's creation and Plan, and are attempting to uplift mankind at this time to a higher level of being in every way, spiritually, mentally and physically. Think on these things and try to achieve whatever you can in the space of time allotted to you. It is most important that man does what he can to make this place, this Earth truly a new Earth and Heaven which has been promised for so long, and will come about in time, I assure you. I give you my blessing this day, to you and all who read these words. God bless, Master Rakoczi.

TEACHINGS FROM THE MASTERS-12

My greetings to you. In this last discourse I wish to speak on several topics, including man's capability of envisaging a new Heaven and Earth, and through these imaginings, how things can be, and by using his mind much can be achieved. Visualisation is a powerful tool as you know, for thought is all powerful, and if you can learn to visualise powerfully, knowing without doubt that something will occur, then gradually things will change upon the Earth and man will be capable of doing this. As you know, all things are possible through Christ, and in having this knowledge within you and using your capabilities to the full, you can bring about many changes for the better within the Earth's structure, man's conditions upon the Earth, and his attitude towards others.

It has to come from within, and if you can gather together sufficient men and women of like mind and work together in this, it is possible for man to work in a brotherhood in this way to bring about many changes for the better, but it must be done with a purity of thought and intent. So many only think of power, and power can corrupt, the power used by Hitler and other subsequent leaders such as the Ayatollah Khomeini who have corrupted to gain power for themselves. It is within the nature of man to want power for himself, but if it is God's power from within you, then no harm can come, only good.

Much has been foretold about the Earth changes, and how there will be devastation and cataclysms occurring at this time, but it is not necessary for this if man will turn to God, and that all mankind tries to join together as one. It has been foretold at other times there will be a new Golden Age, and you should unite to help create what will be a new Earth, so that those who follow you will be provided for, and have some goodness to look forward to instead of violence, evil and negativity which abound at present in so many places.

Attempt to overcome this violence and negativity with pure light and love directly from your hearts, sending forth this energy of love towards these areas where negativity reigns, and only goodness can come from this, for the change within the hearts of men is the most important change to occur. If all of mankind can change, then the Earth changes will not be violent, and gradually man will rise upwards as he is doing at present onto that new dimension. Alongside this, the Earth herself has gradually been altering her dimension, moving steadily upwards, slowly but surely onto the fourth dimension.

It all takes time, and as you know, this time is man made but time is also relevant to this change. Man cannot change in the blink of an eye to be a better, more resilient and ever loving being. It is a gradual thing, and we, the Masters, hope that through our overlighting the Earth in our different ways, we can help you to bring about that change within man. We are ever present, attempting always to send forth our love to mankind. Over the centuries we have incarnated so many times, and mastered everything that you are experiencing now. We understand how it is with you, as we have gone through it ourselves, and overcome all the difficulties that you are facing, and that man has ever faced throughout his generations. We only hope that this time man will take a large step forward into this New Age, this new higher dimension.

All who read this book are spiritually aware, and know now important it is to meditate daily to lift the mind to a higher level and be still; allowing inspiration to come, and knowing this, you can be capable of so much more. Western man has changed to the ways of the East, and gradually more of you are appreciating this time of quiet each day. It is important while stilling the mind, to pray beforehand, so that those who inspire and instil their thoughts are those of the Christ Consciousness. I am sure that all of you are aware of this, but it is important to remember when passing on knowledge, to make others who are newcomers, aware of this.

If all mankind will still the mind each day, and have this peace emanating from within them, filling them with light, then man cannot fail to raise his consciousness and that of his fellow man, so that all of you can work together as one, and work with the Masters to make the world a better place for your children who follow you. A new Heaven and a new Earth, which was promised long ago, and will come to pass before long if you will do your part.

The governments of the world must unite as one, so that there is no great power given to any one country, any one government or any one leader. If all will cooperate in this, then mankind will become as he was when he first incarnated upon the Earth, one with God. We hope that this will come about in the next few decades. We are working to this end, and hope to be proved right in this, our most important work upon the Earth.

This incarnation should be the last for all of you, because once you have achieved reaching upwards towards this higher dimension, then you will be in communication with those who have incarnated, and have passed into spirit. They will be able to show themselves to you quite freely, and you can be in communication with your loved ones.

You will find that as a result, your lives will be altered completely. You will also find that you have more capabilities to allow you to travel quite easily through the power of the mind. Once you have developed this capability, you will no longer need transport as such. As this capability of teleportation increases, you will find that you can transport yourselves through thought wherever you wish, because this is something which man has had latent within him, and which certain men in the Far East who have raised their consciousness are capable of doing to travel great distances. They have achieved many things which man will be capable of in the future once all men achieve this higher vibratory level. You will be able to do many things which would seem miraculous at this time, but as times goes by you will know that it is not truly miraculous, but just another level of being which is there latent within you, and which will be the crowning glory once you have raised into the fifth dimension.

Those presently capable of doing this are living a different life from your own at present within the more built up areas of the world. Most of those who have achieved this capability are living in places far off from here in a more monastic existence. They are Masters who are capable of many things, which you too will be able to achieve as time goes by. They have achieved this through their ability to switch off their conscious minds and become truly inspired, and have increased their capabilities so that they can do many things that would seem impossible at present to you, but they are using their mind as a tool. As I mentioned at the beginning, the mind is all powerful and can achieve many things through God and His power, used for good and through faith in Him, you too can do these things which may in time be very useful, and demonstrate that you can achieve mastery of the mind, body and soul.

Your life on Earth will prove to be a new way of looking at life as time goes by, and if you have a mind to, you can achieve so much, and that you too can in time be Masters of all you survey, but do not feel all powerful in this, but be as little children as Jesus said, in all humility. Then, if you can achieve this mastery over thought, which is all that is necessary, and then you will have done your part in this life to change the Earth to become a better place for those who follow you. I give you my blessing this day, and hope that all of you will be achieving much within the next few years.
God bless and keep you, now and always,
Master Rakoczi.

As was given in book one, we shall conclude with this simple Invocation to the Light, which is powerful, that asks for Michael the archangel to be present.

"Wielder of the Sword of Light come forth.
Defend man from his darkness.
May God's pure Divine Light shine through the hearts of men,
And love and peace prevail."

TEACHINGS FROM THE ASCENDED MASTERS

PART THREE

TEACHINGS FROM THE MASTERS
Book Three

CONTENTS	Page
Section 1 – Master Jesus/Sananda	86
Section 2 – Master Jesus/Sananda	89
Section 3 – Master Jesus/Sananda	91
Section 4 – Master Jesus/Sananda	94
Section 5 – Master Jesus/Sananda	98
Section 6 – Master Jesus/Sananda	101
Section 7 – Master Jesus/Sananda	103
Section 8 – Master Jesus/Sananda	106
Section 9 – Master Jesus/Sananda	109
Section 10 – Master Jesus/Sananda	112
Section 11 – Master Jesus/Sananda	115
Section 12 – Master Jesus/Sananda	118

Channelled by Beryl Charnley

TEACHINGS FROM THE ASCENDED MASTERS-1

This is Sananda. There is so much that I would wish to say to mankind at this moment. My hopes are that times will change for the better. Gradually, imperceptibly I believe there is a change. Not necessarily all over the world, but I feel that there are pockets of people who are increasing their spirituality and attempting to be better citizens, some of them Christians, and this is something that I am pleased to see. All of the Hierarchy are looking for this. There are large numbers of these groups of good people, not necessarily all of the same faith, but all are expanding both their spirituality and their numbers to include others who are waiting in the wings, shall we say, on the verge of learning how they can improve their spirituality and be more evolved individuals. All of you who are spiritually oriented, are attempting to extend and expand your consciousness through meditation and prayer.

There are still 'grey' areas where there is violence, hypocrisy, and where that faith growing within you has been momentarily lost, but I hope in time that even these areas will gradually become golden areas, so their souls will be able to overcome what the lower self is doing at this time. Those who are fighting and those who have had problems for many years, such as Northern Ireland, we hope will be, through faith, uplifted to better things. It is the faith that man must hold on to, the faith that he himself is a spiritual being and one day will blend together with all mankind so that the spirituality of man will be as it once was when first he came upon the Earth, knowing he can speak to God and God can speak to him, which is even more important. In those early days God spoke to all men and it was part of life, it was expected and accepted, but things changed over the years, and man turned aside from God. Now we hope the tide has fully turned and gradually those grey pockets will be filled with faith, and the knowledge that within that still centre mankind will be able to hear God's word, and in hearing that, will turn to serve Him, believing and knowing that this is the pathway for man.

As you know, through faith you can do all things. Faith can move mountains, and if you truly believe, know that whatever you wish can be fulfilled if you have sufficient faith. It is these three things, faith, hope and charity on which I wish to speak. Faith is within each one of you, latent and waiting to be used. Many of you have discovered this and know that if you turn to God and put your troubles in His hands that those troubles will be turned away from you and the problems will be solved gradually, miraculously, if you put your faith in God. It is strange how man thinks that he is alone and that only he is able to solve problems that sometimes seem insurmountable, but if he will have the true faith and just pass those problems to God, forgetting them and allowing Him to solve them then all will be well. Again, 'hope lives eternal' and we hope that man will see this and know that if he truly believes, then the hope that lives within him will also be given credence, and the hopes of all men will be fulfilled. If you were without hope what would life be? It would hardly be worth living if you had no hopes for future happiness. Know that God is always there to give you hope. Pray to Him and ask that your hopes will be fulfilled and truly they will be. If you have the faith to believe, they will, they truly will!

Just allow God to work in His own way. Sometimes it is unexpected in the way in which your hopes are fulfilled, through someone else perhaps who is being used by God for this purpose. Just allow Him into your hearts and lives, and what a change will be wrought. Know that anything can be given to you from God, and if He gives you something, use it and send forth love and gratitude, because everything that is given to you is from God and even though it may appear to be from someone else, your hopes have been granted. Each one of you has different hopes, ideals and needs, but never fear that you expect too much from God. It is needs that are granted, not wants. If someone is truly needy, those needs will be supplied, but if someone is filled with greed and wants something that is unnecessary, then that is not always given to you. It is purely what is necessary that is given, if you wish for something further; then you must supply it yourself. Greed is a different thing from need, and if you will weigh up whether your wants are greed, you will realise that many things are not really required. It is those who truly are needy who have their requirements fulfilled by God. Those whose hopes may feel dashed at the time never despair; you know He is there to help you at all times, so call on Him.

Be charitable to one another too. The words and sayings that have been passed down over the years that 'charity begins at home' are true, because often familiarity breeds contempt, and those you love the most are quite often those who are hurt. Remember that sometimes those who you take for granted and truly love the most and are closest to you can be hurt the most. So be charitable to one another, always remembering the needs of others. Love one another truly and that will make Me truly happy, also because happiness is important. It may seem very fleeting at times, but true happiness is important. It may seem very fleeting at times, but true happiness springs from the heart and that comes from the wellspring within, from God who truly loves you all. Give whatever you can to those in great need. I know that so many of you do give charitably and generously to those groups of people who are suffering at this time throughout the world. The TV programmes that show their suffer is brought into your homes, and you realise how fortunate you are, and you give generously to those charities, and I am sure that what has been received from you will be truly used to advantage.

It is this type of charity that has been spreading over the last few decades. Sometimes more and more of these charities contact you to use your good nature for moral blackmail. Do not be dismayed, for you can only give so much, we know, and if you have this attitude of charity towards others who are suffering, that is all that is required. You cannot do more than you are able. Do not worry or feel pressurised into always increasing the amounts each year. This is not fair to you and you must accept that you can only do your best. God wishes all to have this love and charity to their neighbours but not to the extreme, He does not wish this to happen.

Faith, Hope and Charity, all are important, all involve love, and the greatest of these is Charity. As I said, be charitable to each other, especially those closest to you. God bless and keep you all in His care. Blessings, Sananda.

TEACHINGS FROM THE ASCENDED MASTERS-2

My greetings to you this day, this is Sananda. This is a time of regeneration, of overcoming evil with good and having the confidence to know that through the darkness, light must prevail. There is always light at the end of the tunnel, and the end of the tunnel is nigh. The darkness shall be overcome. If you have the faith to continue with this process, mankind will prevail. There are those who tend to be influenced by negativity and suggest that the end of the world is nigh, and that the earth changes will be very powerful and catastrophic. This is all in the mind of the individual, and if you allow that negativity to prevail, then there would be no hope for anyone, but remember that within you there is that all powerful divine spark which is gradually being fanned to a flame of great incandescence if you will allow this to occur. More of you are waking up to your divinity and spirituality, and this is wonderful. It must be spread abroad.

These words that I give you are most important. I am attempting to spread the word of God to all throughout the world, through channels such as this, so that all may know that they can overcome the evil that is abroad at present. You yourselves are capable of overcoming the negativity in the world, but you must have faith in yourselves and the God within you. God will overcome the havoc through you. You can heal both yourselves and others through having the faith to know that God can work miracles. It may not be immediate, so do not despair. Always realise that God can only do anything that is within your power. If you think about it, it is only through your faith in Him that He can prevail. Therefore the most important thing in your lives is your faith, having the confidence to know, and being convinced that you can do whatever you wish to do through Him.

Think deeply on these words because if you have the will to do something important in your lives, think through it deeply and have the confidence that if you wish to do something, you can do it if you go about it in the right way. Pass it on to God and allow Him to work through you to carry out your purpose, then that purpose will come to pass and what you wish to do will come about, but you must have the confidence to do this work and the capability of carrying it out through Him. Therefore, anything that occurs in the world is through man's realisation that God's purpose can be carried out through Him.

Do not allow power to go to your heads. There are times when this does occur, and has occurred over the millennia. Remember never to feel that you are the one who initiates everything. It is as a result of God working through you that this occurs. No one person should allow power to take over his or her life. There are rulers of men who should use the power they have for the benefit of others, but they should never feel that they themselves are the power because they are not. When I lived my life as Jesus, I never allowed myself to feel that my power was my own. The power within me came from God, the power to cause miracles to occur, to heal, to walk on water, to still the storm, to raise the dead, everything I did was through God, through my faith in Him that I could do these things to show that God was love, and that God so loved the world of men that He sent me to walk amongst men and do His bidding. To show that through my life He could live through men and give His power to them to use for the good of all as I did. My life on Earth was to show that God is love and my love for all continues forever. I am still working in this way to help mankind to overcome the darkness that is upon the world at present. Those who are waking up to their spirituality are beginning to overcome that darkness and will help others to awaken to this power within them and gradually, gradually God, light and love will create a new Heaven and a new Earth.

There are many who are presently questioning how it is in the churches that nothing is changing, that the power of God within each one can be utilised more for the good of others. It seems that the questions are not being answered fully in all of the churches throughout the world, but this matters not, so long as man can use his divinity to help others. It is how you live your lives that is most important. It does not mean that if you go to church each week you can forget about the way you live and the good you can do for others. It is bringing God into your lives and spreading His love and your love unconditionally to all who you meet, helping wherever you can and using His love for all mankind.

Remember that at this time of the year it is a time where goodwill is becoming more apparent. Use that goodwill towards all men at all times of the year, not just at Christmas, and always remember that the Angelic Hosts are close to the Earth, closer than usual at this time. Try to visualise them in your minds, bringing them closer towards you, seeing them surrounding you with their love, and send forth that love to all the dark corners of the Earth where those in need are reaching out for light, love and healing. Give what you can to them and emanate that light to all, the Angelic Light that is hovering near the Earth.

God bless and keep you all.
Sananda.

TEACHINGS FROM THE ASCENDED MASTERS-3

God bless you, this is Sananda. There has been much talk about the Ascension, not My ascension but man's ascension. There have been many versions of this recently and people are confused. They feel that perhaps they are wrong in their beliefs, some thinking they will be lifted up by spaceships, others that they will raise themselves through their own awareness and higher vibration into another dimension through their own consciousness. Some of these versions have been quite garbled, others have been suggesting that the Earth will be in a state of chaos and therefore mankind cannot live upon it. It is time I think to put the matter straight once and for all.

It will be a time of change, that is sure, and changes have been occurring already. Changes in climate, 'you shall not know the seasons,' was foretold, and this has come about already. There have been great winds that have caused devastation. There have been certain parts of the world where there have been earthquakes, floods, and the temperatures have altered in many places throughout the world, resulting in dreadful famine at times, when there had been no rain for many months on end. These things have occurred in the past, but they have been prevailing more recently in a more dramatic way. Man too has changed, some of you have taken a more spiritual path and this is good, but there have been many who have been caught up in violence with people who have been attempting to control others in an extremely aggressive manner without thought for the lives of their own kind.

Now I wish to tell you what will occur, and all mankind is included in this. You must attempt to raise your consciousness so that all of you are able to realise that you can attune to spiritual realms, so that you will be more aware of your minds. The mind is all-powerful, as you know. Thought can inspire others if it is used in the right way. It is hoped that more of you will inspire those who are on the path of negativity, so that light will overcome the darkness. We are attempting to raise the energies of those who are already on the spiritual path, to help you overcome the present world's darkness. You are presently attempting to bring light into the Earth, seeing it as a power for good, and bringing it down towards you and securing it into the Earth.

If all of you who are on this spiritual path will do this twice daily, bringing down that column of pure white light from the heavenly realms, filling your room with this column and rooting it down into the centre of the Earth, so that you are immersed and filled with that light. The light of God, or the light from the Source, whatever you wish to call it, it is power for good and if all of you are filled with that light, every cell of your body is filled with pure white light, then you will help yourself to raise your vibratory level higher as each day goes by. Filled with this light, you can then help others to learn how to raise their consciousness. It is important that this is done each day so that the power of light is secured into the Earth by more and more who are on the spiritual path, spreading this word to others.

As you do your daily meditations, or twice daily preferably, think of that light filling you with great power and spreading outwards into the whole of your aura. As you raise your mind towards the light, going inwards and listening for that still small voice, you will raise your vibratory level, and gradually you will be ready and aware of your higher self. You are bringing your higher self from above, from those chakras in the higher realms into your lower self, so that your whole body is filled with light. This time of quiet each day is of great importance, because your bodies need to be filled with power before they are ready to ascend into the fifth dimension. You are bringing your body into alignment for this, preparing yourselves so that in time many of you will be ready to rise into that dimension so that you will learn to teach others about what is about to occur. As you rise into that dimension, there will be many thousands rising with you, attempting to be the vanguard of those who are ascending.

There will be those who ascend first, who will guide others on their return to Earth. For a while you will cleanse your bodies in that fifth dimension. You will learn much, and will be accompanied by those who will protect and guide you, for you are never alone. I am one who is helping at this time, and those who are assisting Me will be in contact with you also. There are those from other planets who have been helping over the last few decades, who have also been channelling, giving their communications of help and assistance, so that all will understand what is occurring. Those of you who are raising consciousness will not need their help at this time, and are ready to receive the new guidance.

It is difficult to describe, but you will be on another dimension of light. You will be able to see many things that you presently cannot. It is a matter of dimension rather than where you are, you are not rising physically to another point in the heavens, for you will be vibrating on another level. You will still see other people around you, but you will have raised your molecular structure and will not be seen by those around you who are still on the third dimension. As time progresses and you have cleansed your bodies and learnt what it is that is to happen, you will then return to the third dimension and help others who are on the path. You will instruct and guide them. They will be ready to learn because they will understand when they see you returned subtly changed.

I know that you may have heard some of this, but I am trying to make it clearer in a way that you will understand. It is just that your bodies will have transmuted into light and yet you will return without having passed on as souls do when they 'die'. You will return in your normal bodies looking similar to what you did before, but with a subtle difference. You will not have died; within a short space of time you will have passed into light and returned to help. Then the next wave, shall we call them, will be helped and guided and they too will ascend into that fifth dimension. As the Earth is gradually changing, you will find that when you return, you can cope with any changes in the Earth's structure. All will be well and there is much to look forward to when you have changed into your fifth dimensional bodies. There will be many who will not understand this, and who will, unfortunately, have to pass through that transition of death because they cannot accept the new, the new Heaven and new Earth, which will surely come and be better than at present. There is much to go through with violence and conflict as you are aware, but it will not affect you. The changes are there, the seeds of change are there within you now for those of you who will accept these words. I, Sananda, have been trying to help over the past decade or more to explain to those who are ready to accept. Now is the time of change, now is the time to concentrate on light.

As you meditate, visualise a column of light way above your house and bring it firmly down through the roof and into your room to fill you with that powerful white beam of the Christ Light, filling your whole molecular structure, your organs and everything surrounding you, and root it firmly into the Earth below you, sending it right down into the centre of the Earth. This is most important, so that the Earth itself is filled with light from all of you each day, and this will help to change the Earth too, by helping it to rise into the fifth dimension.

Those who work with Me are attempting to channel these words to others throughout the world. It is the truth, for many have heard it, and some are writing books concerning similar truths. I have tried to put it as simply as possible as I, myself, as Jesus, spoke simply and truthfully to those around Me. I hope that this will not dismay you. I am sure that you will realise that things will improve through this light projection, and I know that you wish to help and work in My name, for Me and those around you. I will tell you more in future communications, but for now, God bless and keep you all,
Sananda.

TEACHINGS FROM THE ASCENDED MASTERS-4

Greetings to you this day, it is Sananda. I wish to continue with the Ascension Plan for mankind. It has evolved over the last few years, and is for those who are ready to accept it, it has been laid out and all will then be ready when the time comes. Those already on the spiritual path will be able to take part in this plan, which has evolved gradually, and is for all mankind. Some people have had access to these ideas for a few years, it is usually given to those who are ready to receive and accept it. Do not feel pressurised by this, but just do what is necessary when you feel ready to do so. Accept it or reject it, whatever you feel is right for you at the time.

The idea is to raise your consciousness so that when you begin your meditation each day. See the Star of the Christ shining above you and bring down this shaft of light to fill your room, breathing it in and seeing it pass through you, filling every particle of your being with its light, and see that pure white brilliance pouring down into the Earth below you, securing it into the centre of the Earth, so that the Earth herself can benefit. The Earth is also rising into a higher vibratory level and it is necessary for all who are aware to help the Earth in this way, so that she too can access light from the realms above, this purifying light, which has the power of purifying everything it passes through.

As you bring down this light, visualise your crown chakra opening up as within the rays of the sun like a many petalled lotus flower, and see each chakra of the body opening so that you are ready to receive anything to be given to you from your guide or higher self. You are bringing down your higher self into your lower self, so that you are compacted and can act as one, rather than two halves of the whole. Your higher self can then guide you in any way that is necessary. All of you have access to your higher self in meditation, at times it is as though your guide is speaking to you, a high being, or the God within, but at other times it is your higher self who is guiding you, that self which has incarnated so many times previously, that it has great knowledge stored within.

There have been men in the past who have accessed the fifth dimension, and they are perhaps what you would call miracle workers. I, as Jesus, used this dimension at times when I wished to be alone, when I needed to talk quietly with God the Father. Sometimes I seemed to slip away from the multitude, but actually I had used this capability to pass into a higher vibration so that I could be alone with God and would move secretly away from the area I was in, to a place of peace. Those who have been on a higher level of consciousness have achieved this capability, and it is perfectly possible for this to occur to any who have been meditating for many years. I know that at times there are men who are able to do this at present, for instance, Sai Baba, who frequently has been seen in other places throughout the world when he has actually been talking to many people in his room at his ashram at Brindavan.

I know that he has worked many miracles and caused apports to appear within his hand, as well as vibhuti, which he uses freely. He has made many things happen; healings and miracles that have occurred since he was quite young. This is because he was able to access the fifth dimension from an early age. He and others like him who are high beings presently incarnating have learnt this capability and been able to use this to great effect, to impress on people how it is possible to create miracles, and yet it helps those who worship him to understand that all things are possible through faith. This is something, which I hoped that those who followed me would understand also, and the disciples who accompanied Me had that faith, and were able to accomplish miracles themselves from time to time.

When your reflect on these happenings that have occurred, you will recognise that in time to come when you ascend to the fifth dimension, many things which have seemed mysterious in the past will be made clear. You and all who pass into the fifth dimension will be capable of many more things, and you will be able to help others at this time much more than before. There will be many thousands who are ready and able to pass into this new dimension of being within a short space of time. Believe me, it is the truth and I am attempting to help mankind with the support of many others. As I said, there are those beings from other planets who are helping. Those of Ashtar Command and others who have been guiding mankind over the past few decades to warn him of the changes which are occurring, and which will become more prevalent within the next few years. Just accept my words as the truth and know that before very long you will be capable of transmuting into the fifth dimension.

There will be three sections or waves of ascension for mankind. In the first wave you and others who are ready to accept these words will raise your consciousness and be moved into another dimension. You may feel that you are leaving loved ones behind, but you are not. You will still be here but on a higher vibratory level, and you will return to their dimension within a short space of time. It is purely that you will have speeded up your vibrations and they who are still on the third dimension will not be able to see you. You will learn many things at that time and as your vibrations are raised, you will be slightly changed in your molecular structure.

As a result when you return, you will be able to help others who are on the path but not quite ready, and find that you have capabilities that you did not have previously. Your healing capacity will be much more powerful than before if this is something you feel drawn to, and I think many of you do, if you wish to serve others and God the Father. Other capabilities will be that of telepathy and linking with the two worlds, as many of you already do, channelling teachings of wisdom and guidance for the future for others. As I said before, your bodies will be subtly changed and those who you return to will believe what you say is the truth. I know that it is something, which you feel may never happen, but it will do in time. Everything is gradually changing now, and in time, many thousands will pass into the fifth dimension.

As I have said, you will help the second wave of ascension. You will be guiding them in many ways and I know that you have the faith that you can do all things through Christ, and when this time arrives and the next people are ready to ascend, you will help them to understand what is occurring. Their minds must be prepared through meditation and visualisation. It is most important that meditation is done daily, preferably twice, and at this time the column of light from the Christ Star should be visualised and brought down into their bodies to surround them, rooting the light into the centre of the Earth. This is an important part of the meditation procedure; each one should be advised of this. It is up to anyone to accept or reject it as said. They should try to visualise themselves being bathed in this pure white brilliance from the Christ Star filling every particle of their being. Then they can visualise leaving their room and approaching a stream or river bank, feeling the sun upon them, walking towards that stream, bathing in it and coming out the other side filled with pure white brilliance, so that they are cleansed, and the stream has washed away all their cares, troubles and pain, so that on the other side they are ready for a new beginning.

Visualise ahead a beautiful mountain with the sun shining upon it in the clear air, and feel that you can be there in body, not just in thought, because if you dwell upon this fact you can take yourself to the top of this mountain and look down upon all of the surrounding countryside to see a panorama of beautiful green fields, then drift up into the sky looking down upon the Earth below, knowing that you are safe and shielded from harm. Then gradually float downwards to the mountain top, and return to the riverbank filled with faith, hope and love, walk back into your room and return to your body. You have surrounding you that pure white light which you brought down from the Christ Star that protects you. You can visualise this at any time you wish. It is good to be able to feel that you can do this knowing that all is well. As you return to your body, visualise each chakra closing like a flower. Seal each one with a cross in a circle of light and put a larger cross in a circle of light over your crown chakra after closing it, and then enclose your whole body with a circle of light. This protects you when you return to the outer world. This visualisation is very powerful and will help all those who are attempting to raise their consciousness, so that it will be easy when they ascend to the fifth dimension. It is like a teleportation that is something you will be capable of in the future.

It is good to be able to advise others how to raise their consciousness and how to protect themselves. Visualisations such as these are ideal, and another one would be to visualise stepping into a beautiful bubble of light that appears within your room after you have brought down the column of light from above, and then to float slowly upwards in that protective bubble. Then raise the bubble high into the sky so that you can look down upon your house, then higher still, to see your country, then see the Earth below while you are protected in this pure white light, and project the light down into the Earth from the bubble. Look down and know that all is well; you are travelling safely with your higher self. Then return gently to your part of the world, to your house and room whenever you feel ready to do so. Step out of that bubble and return to the chair you are sitting on, and then to full consciousness, having sealed your chakras as before. These are helpful visualisations for those who need this experience, knowing they will soon be transmuting into the fifth dimension, and will be with you at that time. You can give them the confidence of knowing you will return with them at that future date.

    I have more to tell you in the next chapter of communications, but for now, God bless and keep you all,
Sananda.

TEACHINGS FROM THE ASCENDED MASTERS-5

Greetings to you this day, it is Sananda. I wish to continue with my plan for the Ascension. You are aware that the Earth herself is changing, and these changes within the Earth will become increasingly more apparent as time goes by, as there cannot be changes without some disruption. You are seeing it now with various members of mankind. You know that within the family of mankind, so many of you are attempting to improve your capabilities and evolve your souls through this lifetime, but I am speaking now of those men of violence who will never change their ways and who are causing the name of man to be brought into disrepute. If they do not change their attitudes in a very short space of time, the changes within those areas of the Earth will be more violent, but this should not worry you because by that time you will have raised your vibratory level. You and others like you on the spiritual path will have achieved your transmutation into light, into the fifth dimension, and the Earth herself is gradually rising on to this dimension with your help, with the bringing down of that shaft of light through you into the centre of the Earth.

If each one of you does this daily, then the Earth herself will achieve this in a calmer, easier manner, but there will be physical changes, it cannot be achieved without this. The structure of the Earth is such that the change has to more apparent than that within mankind. Over the centuries since his beginning, man has had a physical body, and it will have to be altered somewhat in its molecular structure, as you are aware before rising into the fifth dimension. It is the same with the Earth, but fortunately for mankind, the changes to be applied to him will be less violent than within the structure of the Earth. It is just a vibratory speeding up, you are aware that many beings of light surround you that you may be conscious of if you can tune into them. You know that they are there in the fifth dimension, but you cannot see them because of the speed of their vibrations. This is how it will be with yourselves, so that once you have raised your vibratory rate sufficiently, the change will occur very fast, within a matter of hours when the time comes, and then you too will be able to see these beings of light surrounding you.

You will be able to see the Devic kingdom in all its glory, everything from the fairy kingdom, the fauns, nymphs, dryads and devas of all sizes, who are made of light, fountains of light. All this will be revealed to you in an short space of time, there is so much to look forward to, a new world will open up before your eyes. Many of you may find this something which you have heard of, but is perhaps unbelievable, but I assure you that this world of beings is very real, much more so than the physical world. Everything is made up of molecules as you know, and this is something learnt while at school. It is just the speed and number of the molecules that varies, as to whether something is solid or not, therefore it should be clear to you that everything is one, but just living at different speeds from one another. Therefore these beings of light are living at a much faster rate than yourselves. It is those who can tune in clairvoyantly and see them perhaps very fleetingly, who know for certain that they exist. Others, like the one who is channelling these words, can tune into them telepathically, unable to see them, but knowing that they are there, and having the faith that the communication comes from them. It is another facet of being, another stream of existence that is there, living alongside you, and which will be revealed to you once you are resonating at their level.

As I have said in previous communications, there will be three waves or divisions of mankind moving into the fifth dimension. The first wave will find it comparatively easy, and will happen within a matter of hours. You will still exist on the physical world, and not pass into spirit, it is just that your physical body will be subtly changed and your very being will become charged with energy. While you are in the fifth dimension many things will be revealed to you as said, and I know that most of you will wish to return to their families and friends, ready to help the next wave of humanity who will join you on the fifth dimension. Those of you who wish to help will return to the third dimension, but continue to exist within both dimensions. It is a matter of knowing that you will have an awareness given to you from the fifth dimension of many extra capabilities that you will find helpful to you and for others who need to know more. You will find that you can heal on a higher level. Healings will take place miraculously at certain times, and you will discover that you know much more than you did previously about many things.

There is so much, that I cannot explain everything in detail. You will be aware that you can raise your vibratory level and return to the fifth dimension if necessary. As you know, this will be speeded up so that it can be done within the blink of an eyelid, and that if you need something on the fifth dimension, you can return and appear to have not moved away from where you were. Perhaps I am not making it plain to you, but as I said in my last communication, this is something that Sai Baba can do, also others who are in incarnation at present, including Mother Meera. I will not mention them all by name, but they are capable of being in two places at once, and it is because they are able to access the fifth dimension that this can occur. You too will have this capability once the time comes, and you will be able to help those on the third dimension in many ways. Therefore, do not be concerned about your family and friends because you will return to them very swiftly after you have ascended to the fifth dimension. It will not seem to them that you have been gone for long, and you will understand when the time comes, and will be able to help them so that they will be prepared and able to accept what is occurring, when the time for ascension comes.

All of you will be safe from any catastrophe that may occur to the Earth, because you will not be on the same dimension as the Earth is at present. You are presently, but once you have reached the next dimension of being, you can remove your physical body for a space of time if there is any danger, and all will be well. The next two waves of people passing into the fifth dimension will have this explained to them. The spacecraft that are hovering nearby the Earth may be needed for the third wave of people, to help from time to time, from beings of other planets eager to help mankind. They will not be necessary for the first two waves who are passing into the fifth dimension, but are there to help and they only wish to do what they can for humanity at this time of change. They too have evolved through this transition period and know how it will be.

Everything will change in the twinkling of an eye. You need have no fear for your loved ones, for all will be looked after. It is only those who have no thought of their own spirituality, and are creating the chaos through wish for power. It is their future, which we are considering now, but we recognise the fact that they will not accept these words as the truth and they will have to pass over to spirit. They will not pass into the fifth dimension like yourselves, but will go onto another planet until they are ready to evolve on to a higher plane of existence; such as Earth will be when she too is on the fifth dimension. There will be a planet ready to accept these people who are not ready to move upwards, who have some evolvement of the soul to accomplish, and will reincarnate onto that third dimensional planet until their souls will accept the truth that is here waiting for you. You have accepted this truth and know the happiness and joy that will come about once you have achieved this step which is quite simple, and which we have been hoping mankind will achieve very soon.

It is a new awakening; it is a new form of life for man, an exciting time to live in that you have chosen for this incarnation to take part in. All will be well. The Ascended Masters of the Hierarchy and all who work with them are helping at this time. God bless and keep you, Sananda.

TEACHINGS FROM THE ASCENDED MASTERS-6

This is Sananda, my greetings to you all. All who read these words are amongst those who will be in the first wave of ascension, and the plan that has been waiting for you for so long. Perhaps some of you are now remembering that secret knowledge within you that only needs to be awakened. As you are aware, you only have to turn within to discover so much. You have heard the words 'Man know thyself and thou shalt know the Universe'. This phrase has been given to mankind throughout the ages and it is the truth. There are already a certain number of you who have this knowledge and who are re-establishing it within your conscious mind. It only takes a little seed to be planted within you and the knowledge will blossom and flourish, and you will be able to pass on that wisdom to others around you. Now is the time of awakening, your soul is ready and able to accept these words. I know that some of you may have doubts, and that is only human, but the time will come when we will begin this new plan for mankind and I promise you that all will be well.

It is like a step into the unknown, I know that, and sometimes it may be that you feel it is a faltering step, but no, you have the capability and you have been aware for some time that your purpose here in this incarnation is to evolve spiritually, to be able to raise your consciousness to a new level of awareness, and this is in order to be able to rise into the fifth dimension easily. As I have said it will just be a matter of hours, and you know that during that time your physical body will change very slightly. It is difficult for you to accept this, but it will be so and all will take place quite easily for you. You may be aware that large numbers of you have dwelt on other planets in past lifetimes. There have been those who have received channellings from these planets in the same way as the one who has channelled these words, and has received communications from two other planets, one of which she incarnated on several lifetimes ago.

Many of you have had lives elsewhere, and have knowledge within you, that presently you are unaware of, but once you have ascended, you will remember all that you have within you from that previous lifetime on another planet. Most of the planets that you have incarnated upon are those who have contacted humanity over the last few decades, such as the Pleiades, Arcturus, and many planets that have been helping over the millennia, like Sirius. There are several planets involved that I have not mentioned, but I know that you recognise these names from information now available. It is difficult to say within one communication how these planets are involved with the Earth. I incarnated on Venus in the past, and others of you have also incarnated there. It seems an unlikely planet to have lived upon, but you know that everything is different upon these other planets. The life forms are different, and occasionally those life forms are not living upon the planet but within it, and therefore one cannot assume that life is non-existent there.

So many scientists in the past have worked out the temperature, climate and wind-speed, and deciphered this from the space probes, and presumed that it is completely impossible for beings to live upon these planets, but they have not perceived the fact that life can be in many forms as you know, either liquid, gaseous or other ways that you cannot imagine. I will not go into detail on this, but just remember some of the programmes on television that have opened your eyes to the fact that humanoids are not the only beings which inhabit the Universe. In future times you may realise and eventually meet many of these beings from other planets, because they are waiting to help mankind at this transition into the fifth dimension. There have been many books written in what you call science fiction that have been inspired by those who have written them. This inspiration has come to them from beings who have lived, or are living on the planets, and have been described by them.

There is much communication between planets, and between them and the Earth. The transport of the craft between the various planets is not as you might imagine, for they are not using fuel as you know it, but mainly through the power of thought plus other methods, these vehicles of light move between planets. Vast distances can be covered in the twinkling of an eye, and mankind has much to learn in this way. The vehicles that he has used are extremely powerful, and through much scientific discovery over the last few decades, man has been launched into space. In future, once the Earth and humanity have risen to the fifth dimension, the vehicles will be vastly different from those used present, because the gravity will not have to be considered, and so many more things will be possible when this occurs. The Earth herself is changing and although some changes may be quite cataclysmic at times, there will be a new generation of life on Earth.

After the changes, you will discover that new lands have been formed and the changes brought about will be remarkable, as the Earth will have changed in dimension. Therefore the changes will be subtly beautiful, and you will find that having discovered your capability of seeing the Devic kingdom, they too will be delighted that you can join with them in the work ahead, to found a completely new Earth, and begin a new life of activity within the realms of light that has been brought into your vibratory level. You will see colours that at present you could not imagine, and the Earth will be beautified to a level that is only accessible in dreams! All will be well. There is much to look forward to in future days. We are taking care of everything for you, for your children and your children's children. God bless and keep you all, Sananda.

TEACHINGS FROM THE ASCENDED MASTERS-7

This is Sananda, and I give you my greetings this day, and continue with my Ascension plan for mankind. Perhaps you may not have thought of this concept, do you realise now that in ascending to the fifth dimension in this way, your bodies will be changed forever? It is a perfectly painless procedure. All this has come about through God's Plan and He is protecting you in everything that occurs, so do not fear anything. Your bodies will be so changed that there will be no transition of death in future days for mankind. I say death, because nothing dies at all, as you know, it just passes into another dimension, but this time you are passing into another dimension and yet your bodies are still a part of you. You will exist on both dimensions for some time, until the Earth herself has changed and transmuted into the fifth dimension, like yourselves.

Therefore it is a new thought, a wonderful thought, that in future there will be no suffering. As a result of this change, your bodies will not age, and they will gradually return to the prime of life if you are past that, as it would have occurred when passing into spirit. But this time you are taking a giant step forward, it is completely new uncharted territory for you. As I transmuted into light, so will you, and the change in your outlook should be one of expectancy, hope and happiness, because you will never be parted from one another even for a few days. Instead of the gap between the transition of one of you into spirit, there will be nothing like that in the future. You will not be parted from your loved ones, and therefore this new thought will be something to look forward to in future days. God's Plan has been well thought out. It has been in the process for a long time, and mankind will find that he has a new life ahead of him.

Those of you who have already been in soul contact by meditating for some years and on the spiritual path, you will have now accepted this plan. It may be difficult for others to come to terms with it. If they cannot, that is all right, do not worry, it is there for all, and it will occur in due course, and in time they too will come to accept these words as the truth, which they are. It may be that you are not quite ready and feel that it may not come to pass, just reject it for the time being, and carry on with your life. This is what you all must do in any case, but the meditation is part of your lives now. Something that you always do, that upliftment of your mind to the realms above, and the listening and turning within that gives you some time of quiet, and helps you through your daily life. It is a time of peace even if you do not hear your inner voice, and is a time that you set aside for that peace and quietude. Others may not be ready for this, but the time will come when they will feel this need to be in contact with the realms above, with God, and they will recognise the fact that they are a part of Him as all living things are.

We know that you are accepting the fact that all of us, the Masters of the Hierarchy, the Archangels Michael and Gabriel, and those who are helping us from the other planets, particularly Ashtar, who is one who has been of great help to us, all of us are working in conjunction to make sure that this Ascension Plan comes about very smoothly in the years to come. You will find that in time, you will relax and be ready to accept whatever occurs. After all, it is only like walking into another room, and will be as simple as that, and you will be prepared when your time comes, to transmute into this new dimension. Your guide, your inner voice, that God within will instruct you and be with you at that time. It will be like stepping through a lighted doorway, through a corridor of light, and you will find that others are there, excited awakened beings who are ready and willing to accept these words.

Many of your friends will be with you and you will return in a very short space of time to your loved ones, who will hardly have noticed that you have gone, for as you know, the time between the two dimensions can stretch forwards and back, so that it may appear that you have been gone an hour or two at the most. The two dimensions are interlinked, and you will find that all will be as you left it. It is not as though you are passing into spirit, you are already spirit, passing into another dimension, virtually here and now. You will just disappear temporarily.

If you have practiced the visualisations that I gave you previously, and perhaps enlarged on those, you will find it quite easy to accept, because for instance, if you step into the bubble of light and float upwards, you can conceive of yourselves looking down upon your house, rising upwards and looking down on the countryside round about, and rising higher so that you look down upon your country, and then upon the whole Earth in time, still safe in your bubble of light. That bubble of light represents your light body that is part of your etheric that surrounds you, and intertwines throughout your whole physical body. Your light body is virtually the spirit within you, and it is that which is rising upwards looking down, rather as when you are dreaming while asleep. Your spirit can soar wherever it wishes into the astral, the fourth dimension, still attached to your body by the silver cord, so that you are quite safe and can travel wherever you wish. It is the same principle that we are talking about. Your whole spirit and soul are linked with your physical body, and you are just moving into another dimension, and then returning to the third dimension quite simply.

If there are any doubts in your mind, practice these visualisations regularly. Perhaps you have other favourite ones that you can use. Visualisation is a powerful tool for the mind, and it helps you to appreciate what will be occurring. I know that some of you have not done visualisation or perhaps cannot picture things very easily in your mind, but if you work at it and try to imagine yourself walking along a beach in the warmth of the sun doing something that you have done physically, and can visualise from a past holiday. Think of this, see your footprints in the wet sand and see the water flowing towards you and retreating. The sound of the gulls and of children at play, all these things can make it real for you, so that your visualisation becomes stronger, and therefore your thoughts become stronger. It is through thought that many things can be done, and through thought that you can achieve many things that you could not have imagined possible. As you know, you can send forth healing thoughts to others and positive thoughts to those who are about to take a journey, wishing them well. It is like a prayer and these visualisations can help you on your way.

Those of you who are happy with these thoughts and are ready for this plan will be accepting everything, knowing that all is well and they will return to help the second wave who are on the verge of understanding. You will be teachers and guides to them all, and they will accept your words as the truth because you will have more power behind you. You will have achieved that capability which some have now, those who are very powerful healers, those who counsel others, and you yourselves will be as they are, able to counsel and guide people when they are afraid. All who are in the second waves of humanity will find it quite simple and will rise on to the fifth dimension very easily when the time occurs, and return if you wish to the Earth. I am sure that everyone will feel that they will be starting a new life on this new Earth, which will be changed to a beautiful place of peace. There will be no wars, and mankind will live as once he did when he first inhabited the Earth, peacefully and working alongside the animals as a friend, not an enemy, not killing animals as some do at present, but he will be as he once was, at peace with all.

The third wave of ascension will take a little longer, and although there may be help required, all will take place smoothly when the time comes. There will be so many others who have returned, ready to help those who have not already passed into the fifth dimension, and spacecraft will be waiting if it is necessary for some to be lifted onto those craft.

Change is all about you, but it will be a change that will be for the good of mankind, and the good of planet Earth, and a new life awaits in future times. Many prospects that you had not imagined will occur, and all will be well. Without change there is no progress, and man should accept that he will find change stimulating and always attempt to progress upwards in his lifetime, there should never be stagnation. There should always be a change for the better. All is well. All is very well. God bless and keep you all,
Sananda.

TEACHINGS FROM THE ASCENDED MASTERS-8

My greetings to you this day, this is Sananda. I hope that you are not disturbed by the thought of this large step to be taken by mankind. If you cannot accept this truth for what it is, put it away for some time in the dark recesses of your mind. Just reject it for the time being and continue with your life's work, whatever you feel is right for now. It is true that it is something that is for the future, but if you think of it in the present, when that time comes, you will be able to accept it more readily. It is something that is quite simple and can be accepted by all when the time comes, but for the moment, I know that some of you feel that you cannot accept this and hope it is something that will not occur. Do not feel this way because it is God's Plan for mankind, it is an easy way out, in other words. You do not have to suffer the pangs of that transition you call death; there will be no death in the physical sense. You are just passing into a new dimension quite painlessly, particularly if you meditate and use the visualisations that I have given you, and others of which I am sure that you are aware. It will be a simple thing that will occur almost in a twinkling of an eye, so accept these words for what they are meant, just to make it easier for you.

As Jesus, I used to say, 'I am the Light of the World, you are my light in the world', and you will be spreading my words to others when the time is right. You are the Second Coming, shall I say. It has always been said, there will be a Second Coming of the Christ. You, when the time comes will be that Second Coming, you yourselves will be Christed Ones when you have passed into that other higher dimension, and you will be capable of so much more than you could imagine. As you know, you are already beings of light, with that divine spark within you, and the more that you bring down light from the Christ Star, the more you will be filled with light and act as one with your higher self.

Therefore, you will become a light network rather like electricity. It sounds rather mundane, but imagine the whole world with each country having within it that grid of electricity that lights up each town and city like a network throughout the world. This is how you lighted beings will be shining your light towards others, and upwards to join with us in the realms of light, so that we become one, and there will no longer be that veil between us. You will be a part of the realms of light, without having to pass through the transition of death. You will be linked with us, having raised your consciousness to a higher level of awareness and be as one with us. This is what we hope for mankind in time, so we can all work together as one for the good of the whole.

In the past, man has been a lonely creature, he has felt separated from his God except in times of prayer, and except for those who are aware that they can be conscious of God through their minds, linking in meditation to hear that still small voice. There is no separation any longer, and man will be linked always with that divinity within, once he takes that step into the fifth dimension and ascends. All of you are capable of much more than you are aware, as I have told you before. You will link with one another through thought once you have taken that step, and you will be able to speak to one another through your minds. Certain people can do this already, who are linked with God, and have raised their consciousness to a higher level and are aware of that still small voice constantly. Most of these of whom I speak are already in the fifth and third dimensions, like Sai Baba, Mother Meera and other sainted beings as was Mother Teresa. It may not have occurred to you that already certain members of your society have taken that step, and they may appear to you as you appear to them and to each other, no different because they are still physical, and this is how it will be when the time comes for you too to take that step, that ascension. You will be working on both dimensions, as I have said previously, for some time to come, until the Earth herself has also fully moved upwards.

Try to develop unconditional love within yourselves, so that you can gather towards you others who are feeling lost and lonely, who perhaps are worried about the coming changes on the Earth. As you have already realised, these began some time ago and are more apparent now, with flooding, earthquakes, volcanoes erupting more frequently, drought and changes within the whole climate of the world. All this was foretold and you are accepting this, but there are some who are fearful and these are the ones for whom I speak. You can help them through a word here and there, and try to make them realise how important it is to meditate and have that link with the higher realms. Most of these people have been aware of prayer all their lives, but not necessarily meditation, which as you know has always been practised in the eastern countries more than in the west, and is only recently that the west has integrated it into life, to listen as well as speak to God. He has much more worthwhile thoughts to give you than you might have imagined was possible!

Most of you who read these words have been meditating for some time, but I am just attempting to reinforce this message, that the higher you can reach upwards with your consciousness, the easier it is to accept everything that will occur in future days. Your links will become stronger and that light that is pouring down from the Christ Star will help to strengthen your faith.

I said in my last communication that this is a time of great change, and that humanity should be aware of this and be ready to adapt and accept it. Be flexible and know that change is good. All these changes within the Earth are good and cleansing. It may not appear so, but when the time is right and you are ready to take this step, you will appreciate how good these changes are, and how it was necessary, so that those men of violence and evil will be swept aside when the Earth changes become more prevalent and things change for the better in every way. The whole of the Earth will be beautified, resurrected, and it will be a golden age of peace once you have passed that transition into the light together with the Earth. All this change will happen gradually, and it should be a time of great fruitfulness for man in a way that he has not perhaps thought. You are to be given the opportunity of new gifts, of healing and great power of speech in counselling others. Once you have ascended to that new dimension you will be Masters in the making, you will be given capabilities and powers that you could not imagine at present.

As you are aware, I was and still am a Master. While I was Jesus the Christ I was capable of doing many miraculous things in that lifetime. I was able to constantly link with God as you are aware, receiving His words and His gifts that you will be given, perhaps not to the same extent as I was, but you will be abundant in these gifts and use them for the good of others when that time comes, I know that you will wish it. You are changing even now physically in different ways. It may be that you have been aware of pain of some kind, even fleeting pain. This is all part of the changes in your molecular structure, and the Earth too is changing in different ways as mentioned with the flooding, earthquakes and drought; all these things are to be taken into consideration as part of God's Plan. Accept this and realise it is for a purpose and all will be well. Have faith and know that everything that happens will be for the good of mankind, for his future and future generations to come who will dwell upon a green and pleasant land. All will be well and you have much to look forward to.

God bless and keep you all, Sananda.

TEACHINGS FROM THE ASCENDED MASTERS-9

I give you my greetings this day, this is Sananda. I hope that all of you are feeling filled with light, that light from the Christ Star, because the more that you bring down into your homes and your hearts, the more easily you will become Christed beings once you take that step into the fifth dimension, that ascension of mankind. Over the time that I have been giving these teachings I have been attempting to free you from your physical restrictions which all have while in incarnation. It is a question of freeing the mind, accepting the fact that through visualisation you can achieve so much. The more that you practise visualisation yourselves, in that bubble of light drifting upwards into the heavens, the more that you can realise how you will feel once you have ascended onto that fifth dimension. You will be able to travel wherever you wish, using your mind as a tool. Think of that and how wonderful your life is going to be in the future! If you can imagine yourself in that bubble of light looking down on the Earth, you can then picture how things can be once you have achieved this new dimension.

All will be well, you will be protected constantly. Do not think that you will just drift off and not be able to return. As you know, you cannot do this, you are permanently attached to your physical body even whilst asleep, and all the more so when you consciously visualise this bubble of light; that is your protection. It is God's Plan for mankind that he will join with us truly to become one, working together between the two dimensions and gradually raising the whole of mankind into a new awareness. Expanding their consciousness so that mankind is truly a being of light. Those who do not accept these words of truth will not become one with us, and will not continue into that new dimension, and will pass into spirit and not be a part of the new Heaven and new Earth. It is only those who will accept these words both now and in future days who will be ascending.

There are many who at present are not upon the spiritual path, but are good people who live their lives and are loving towards one another; they have not yet reached the point of learning that meditation should be a part of their lives. This is perfectly all right and gradually in time they will be accepting these words and consciously attempting to change their lives to fit in with this new concept. It is just something that they have not known about previously, but they will be ready and able when their time comes and all will be as one. It is only those of evil intent and are unacceptable that will be swept aside when the Earth changes come to pass. As said, the changes within the Earth are already upon us, but it is at the time of more dramatic change coming about that it will be necessary to be upon the fifth dimension.

I know all of this takes some accepting, and gradually most of you are coming round to this way of thinking. After all, your lives have been normal up to now, the way that you have been brought up in past years, and conditioned to more strict religious beliefs. This is now part of the New Age of spirituality that has come to pass over the past few decades and is gradually spreading. More and more people are turning to this new way of thinking, in the new age of Aquarius, when there has been a change in the attitude of so many to their spiritual awareness. Most of you feel that you are part of a secret service. You have your normal everyday existence living as you have always done, meeting up with friends and acquaintances and you cannot pass on this great new wisdom to them, which you are longing to shout from the rooftops. Then you meet up with those of like mind and you can confide in one another, and talk endlessly about how the changes will come to pass, and how your lives are changing dramatically for the better. It is only when you can speak freely that you can feel that you are living life to the full.

It is hoped that in time you will be able to pass on this knowledge to those acquaintances who so far you have felt it was impossible to confide in. Try to reach out to them to shed some light in their lives, I know that you long to do this, but it is difficult to broach the subject. It is important that as many can be confided in as possible. It takes some courage I know, and you feel that perhaps if you broach this subject too soon or at the wrong time, that the friendship with them would end. Certainly some friendships will end slowly but surely, when you realise that you have little in common now, so it just comes about naturally without any hurt or hindrance. They just come to an end, but hopefully you will make new friends and acquaintances who will be of like mind. I know that many of you meet together in groups, working together, meditating and discussing things of interest for the future, many teachings that you have read in other books, comparing notes. All this is good because it helps you to feel more confident about the changes that are occurring in the Earth and in yourselves in so many ways.

I have told you how you will be working between the two dimensions once you have taken that step into the light. There will be so much more power that you will receive into your bodies, and your vibratory level will have risen quite considerably, so anything that you attempt to do will be much simpler once you have accessed that other dimension of light. It is just like stepping through a doorway of light, and you will find many friends and loved ones inside it who are also joining you on that dimension and ascending with you. It is not a question of rising into the heavens, in fact, but raising your vibratory levels, and expanding your consciousness so that you can accept the new capabilities that you will have. You are aware that the beings from other planets are helping at this time, and you know they too will be visible to you in the future. They are waiting with eager anticipation for you to be able to see them as they see you.

They too are evolved beings, not as evolved as the Masters of the Hierarchy, but much more than those on Earth in the third dimension. They have existed on the fifth and sixth dimensions for many years. They do not have time as you do, they do not work with the time concept, and once you have passed into that new dimension, you too will understand this, your minds at present are finite and cannot conceive how they can exist without time. It is difficult to describe, it is something you must accept and have faith in, and once you have reached that stage you will realise how restricted your outlook has been in the past, as all men have been. It is not your fault, it is just a fact, and once that stage has been reached, you will understand many things that at present seem to be a mystery. You will be able to cause things to happen which I cannot describe to you at present, but one is that you will be able to travel instantaneously through the mind, which at present would be miraculous to you, apart from your visualisations of travel, you yourself will then be able to travel bodily and arrive quite simply in the place that you wish to be, with no transport required.

The molecular structure of your bodies will be altered gradually, but once you have reached that dimension of light, your bodies will be completely different while on the fifth dimension, and you will be able to reach out towards us and join with us, working together in your body of light. It is rather like while asleep in dreams, you can rise up and fly through space at an incredible rate. You can imagine from your dreams of flying that you probably have actually done this, your astral body travelling in the fourth dimensional astral plane, able to move wherever you wish. This will come to pass truly, once you have ascended.

The Earth herself is changing slowly but surely, it will never move away, remaining in this orbit always, with the other planets in the solar system. She is just taking that giant step into the higher dimension and joining with those other planets that are on a higher level. As I have said, I have incarnated on Venus, and many others of you have incarnated either on Venus or other planets that are in the higher dimension. You will find that the Earth will be changed and become a beautiful place. It still is beautiful in many parts, but the pollution will be gone and many features will change. Where there is presently desert will become fertile once more, and mountainous regions may change to become more level plains. All this is for the future and you will be perfectly safe while these changes happen. It will happen quite quickly because by that time there will be no time. So do not concern yourselves because you will be safely on that higher level, and when it is safe to return, in the twinkling of an eye all will be well and you can return to the new Earth to take your place in society once again.

All will be well. Have faith and know that all will happen as it is meant to, in God's Plan for man, and that new Heaven and new Earth that was promised so long ago will come to pass. God bless and keep you all,
Sananda.

TEACHINGS FROM THE ASCENDED MASTERS-10

This is Sananda, I give you my greetings this day, and hope that all of you are accepting my words as the truth, feeling filled with light from your meditations. I know that some of these new thoughts that are being given may seen strange to you, but just read them and either accept or reject them, though that seed thought is now in your minds and you are also awakening to the fact that you are all workers for the light and have been for so long. You have forgotten what you are capable of and it is necessary to awaken each one of you to your capabilities. They may be latent, but they are there within you, and in time you will learn to use them; in the meantime, just allow yourselves time and continue with your lifestyle as it is at present.

There is so much that will happen in the future, which is great news and something to be looked forward to. There is no dread involved, just love, light and perfection. Think of the world being a place filled with peace and with people who will tolerate and love one another for what they are. There will be no one wishing or seeking for power to dominate others. All of you will be as one and equal, as you truly are and God thinks of you all as equal. Remember this and know that you are all worthy of His love. His plan for you is unfolding like a flower, it is something that perhaps works slower than you might expect, but slowly and relentlessly, everything will unfold as it should. Allow God to work in His own way, it may not be in the way you would expect, but He has His plans for the Earth and all that dwell upon it, and He is working His Plan out through us, through the Ascended Masters, the Angelic Hierarchy and Michael, and also Ashtar and all who work with him. We have been working together for so long, and the plan is working itself out.

I have said that there will be three waves in this Ascension Plan. There is an ever-increasing amount of new energy coming to Earth which will be working upon you without your knowledge, and gradually, imperceptibly, you will begin to accept and realise that these changes are all for the better. The Earth herself has been changing as you are aware, and all the earthquakes and floods are more apparent and frequent as time progresses. Our planet is gradually rising to the fifth dimension with you, so she will join with those other planets in the solar system and other universes around which are on that level. You are aware that there is so much more than you can see in the heavens above and beyond, because the universe is gradually spreading, constantly evolving and never ending, rather like your consciousness rising and expanding, so everything changes gradually, growing and evolving as it should.

Nothing can remain static, there is always change and this is good. Just think of nature itself, the seasons come and go, and change happens all the time. There is inner growth that you cannot see occurring in the winter, rather like your inner life that is expanding and growing as your soul evolves. Over each incarnation it grows and expands and learns so much, and this is good because that is what life is for, the evolvement of the soul, and that inner life that is becoming more apparent and extending into your daily existence during your meditations. All this is part of the growth of mankind into a new spirituality, that had been lost and now is found within each one of you, and hopefully within many more as they slowly awaken and become aware that they are beings of light.

What is necessary at this time, is for you to attempt to reach upwards, always trying to extend your capability of listening with your inner ear to that still small voice that will communicate and guide you on your way. Continue with your visualisations and improve on them if you can, so that your consciousness will expand even further. Perhaps together you can help one another, you, your families and friends, in groups, so that you can experience the power gathering within that group, that energy which is being poured down with the light into you and the Earth, so that life will become easier for each one of you at this time. You are making history because mankind has never before been so close to such a wonderful new horizon. It is a time of awakening. It is a time for new frontiers to be broken through and extended. There is a dam burst of light pouring down to give you new hope, new life and new joy, because that is what you will receive once you have crossed that threshold into the fifth dimension. It is just like stepping across a threshold into light into a wonderful new world in which you can do so much more than you have ever done in your lives, than any man has ever done apart from those who are already in the fifth dimension and above, like myself and the other Ascended Masters, I am speaking of mankind in general.

It is what God has planned for mankind, He gave you free choice and this is something that those on other planets have not had. The Angelic Hierarchy does not have free will, they live to serve God and they are beings of light who have always served God and mankind over the aeons, but I am just trying to explain to you that you have had free will and now are being given a greater freedom of body, mind and soul. You have experienced in your visualisations that freedom of spirit that you are only aware of while you are asleep in dreams, but from now onwards you will have that capability. All this has been planned for so long, and even though most of you are beginning to accept this truth that you have been awakened to now, it has been 'on the cards', shall we say, for such a long time that we are hoping that more people will be told of this plan.

The Devic Kingdom is also working with us and is ready to help you in their own way. All of us are joining together to raise the natural environment onto that higher dimension. You will find that everything will be perfectly normal and your bodies will adjust accordingly, quite simply and easily. Do not concern yourselves too much with thinking you must stock pile food, water, and provisions of all kinds. There should be no panic or panic buying. There is no need for this because your bodies will adjust, and your needs will be less. As the Earth changes occur, you will be on that dimension of light, so all will be well, and when you have returned you will find that everything will adjust and be as you would wish it to be, with no problems of flooding or earthquakes, so everything will be protected, including your homes. All of you will be in the right place at the right time, and your loved ones will be protected. No harm will become any of you, and you have so much to look forward to, so much peace, happiness and goodwill will abound upon the Earth, and life will be as it should be.

I hope that all of you will accept these words, because in time to come your lives will be changed, for instance, you will find travelling methods that you have only dreamt about previously. There will be travel between the planets, also in ways that will be inconceivable to you at present. The spacecraft that have been travelling from your planet Earth to various points within the solar system will not be required in the future. You will find that the vehicles of light available for you will be faster, simpler, and travel without the use of fuel used in the past. You will understand of what I am talking when the time comes, and you will recognise that all the plans that have been laid for future space vehicles will not be needed. There will be a simplicity of life that you will be happy and willing to accept. There will be much time to enjoy with your families, and time to visit others who live at great distances, but the travel will happen within the space of a few minutes instead of many hours.

The changes will be wrought within time, and as a result your lives will be lived in a different way from presently, it will be in a way in which you will find great relief from the pressures that at present abound in the world. There will be no stress, and disease will be a thing of the past. All will be well. God bless and keep you all, Sananda.

TEACHINGS FROM THE ASCENDED MASTERS-11

This is Sananda and I give you my greetings this day. I hope all of you are feeling very blessed at this new development in the history of man, because it is a time of a new release of energy that is accelerating the learning and development of man's spirituality. There is a great expansion of consciousness at this time, and I am sure you are aware that you are being given help in accepting the news of the ascension of man. Think of how it will be in future days when there will be no transition of death or suffering of any kind. Mankind will be spared this and he will be immortal as such, without the transition or suffering that I went through for mankind at that time as Jesus the Christ. All of you will have a new reality that has always been there, but has been veiled by the illusion of materialism.

The physical world is real to you while you are incarnating, and yet your inner spiritual life is the true reality that has existed over the millennia since man first incarnated upon the Earth. That spiritual life that has always been there within you, and which some are completely aware of and have nourished, fulfilling their evolvement of the soul, but there are very many who have not done so. Perhaps some of them are good people, but are unaware of the importance of their spirituality; they will be helped through this time and you can guide them. This is part of your evolvement, to be helpers, teachers and guides once you have crossed the threshold of light and transmuted into the fifth dimension, returning to help those setting out on the path to pass into their true reality, so that they too are ready to ascend.

The first ones of the three waves, who have awakened from their dream, the 144,000 who awoke to their responsibility at the Harmonic Convergence in August 1987, many of you discovered the true reality, and many energies have been pouring into the Earth since. The gateway was opened when many of you helped to create it by appearing at significant points upon the Earth at dawn and other times over that weekend. These energies have been working on you and all mankind, attempting to help you recognise what tasks you will do and what your task is for your incarnation. It was a time that you chose to be upon the Earth, and many of you have now taken this to heart and are serving God and mankind. Attempting to raise your consciousness and meditating twice daily, bringing down the Christ Light into the Earth and filling yourselves with that light.

Spread these words to all who are ready to accept them. They must have open minds and hearts in order to receive, but I feel sure that within the next few years many more will have awakened to their true reality. There is much to be done at this time. It is a time of great exhilaration and excitement for those who have recognised what is about to occur. You have recognised that this is an historic time in the life of humanity, and I am sure that as these energies continue with their work within you and the Earth, that the changes will come about smoothly and easily. You are aware that when your moment comes to pass into the fifth dimension, that you will see a lighted doorway and when ready, join with others who are ready to pass through that threshold of light.

Probably you have been attempting to envisage this doorway that will help you when the time comes. You have been using visualisations of various kinds, and in this way it helps you to be relaxed and ready to accept your new reality. I know that many of you wish to pass through the doorway together, and if you meditate together this will occur at the right time for all of you. Some of you have already passed into that doorway and exist on the two dimensions simultaneously. Those who have been aware of this information and accepted it some time ago have already passed over that threshold and are helping others to understand what is to occur. I know that those who have done so are impatient and eagerly awaiting the transference of their friends, relations, and any others on the spiritual path to join them in this new life.

There is so much to look forward to for mankind in future days, I have told you that you will be able to cause miracles to occur, particularly in healing, and this is what we are expecting from all of you. That you will wish to help others through this transition, and at times when people are suffering you will be able to relieve their symptoms in a much more powerful way than previously. There will be an authority about you that you have never had previously, which very few men and women have had in the past, because you will have abilities that are beyond your ken. Beyond the average ability of anyone incarnating at this time, apart from those already passed over that threshold of light. I experienced this capability when I became The Christ, when I was Jesus, but you too will be Christed ones. Once you have recognised this, you will be ready to become powerful and capable beings of light.

What is necessary at this time is for you to have faith and patience, and the confidence to know that you are being helped by other beings of light through this time. You have your Guide and Guardian Angel with you always, and all of us within this group of beings of light, myself Sananda, the Master R who is also Comte de Saint Germain, Michael, Gabriel, Ashtar and so many others. We, the Ascended Masters are the White Brotherhood, it is another name for us but we are one and the same, all of us are helping mankind through this transition and only wish for you to open your minds and hearts to everything that will be occurring, and make it easier for yourselves to pass into this new dimension of being.

As I have said before, energy and light are pouring into the Earth from the heavens above at this time, and the more that you accentuate this light by bringing it down through you into the centre of the Earth and root it there, the more you will be helping to accelerate the Earth to accept these energies and make it easy for the Earth herself to pass through this transition stage into the fifth dimension, so that there will not be too much turmoil and devastation. This will be occurring more in the areas where there is violence, greed and lust for power, so do not concern yourselves unduly about the changes within the Earth because you and your loved ones will be cared for and protected.

The time of awakening is now. Put your trust in God and allow yourself to expand in your consciousness; do not restrict yourselves, but visualise with a new awareness what your capabilities will be. Your consciousness will be boundless and you will be able to link with the Universal Mind and with all those who link with it, so that you will receive all knowledge. You will know the wisdom of the Ancients and be able to achieve greatness, not for yourselves individually, but for all humankind and all who are within the cradle of humanity. You and other like you will care for everything upon the Earth, and those who are dependent on you. Everything that lives on the Earth is in that cradle, and the God within you will expand and you will have that unconditional love which you have been attempting to achieve for so long. I will be with you always. I give you my blessing this day, Sananda.

TEACHINGS OF THE ASCENDED MASTERS-12

God bless, this is Sananda. You are aware that the time is nigh for mankind's awakening to a new awareness of his spirituality, and many of you have already awakened to this. It is true that it is difficult to accept this capability that you will have in the future, this Ascension Plan for mankind that has already begun. So many of you feel ready to accept it, and feel it is a wonderful time in the history of man, a time of great excitement. It is as though you are standing on the brink of a new life, which you will be, because once you have reached the fifth dimension you will be capable of blending with the Cosmic Consciousness, and capable of miraculous deeds that you may find necessary to prove to those who are on the point of awakening, that this is their true reality also. It takes time to digest these new thoughts, and I know that there are some who cannot accept them yet, but there has been that seed thought planted in their minds that can be stored away until the time when they are ready to accept this plan that will come about in due course.

It is very difficult to put a time limit on anything since so much depends on how man is reacting. If there is a change in the hearts of those who are presently at war, there will be a new attitude to peace, so that the problems that may be expected to arise from the Earth changes may not be so disastrous as you might imagine. If man will be more tolerant and less power mad in these areas, then the changes will be smoother and more peaceful for all. I feel that man being what he is and always has been in the past, except for the true beginning of man when he first appeared on the Earth, that there have always been wars and rumours of wars since then. As a result, there will be more dramatic happenings within the Earth of further volcanic action and climate changes. You have already discovered that the seasons have become confused, so that wintertime has spring-like or summery days within it.

All this is occurring world wide and some areas are finding that the winters are severe with temperatures dropping to an all-time low, and other areas have unbearable heat, and still more parts of the world, of course, has the flooding we know only too well. All this has come about because the Earth herself is changing slowly but surely, rising to that higher dimension. Everything changes, nothing stays the same in any lifetime, change is good and you have found that imperceptibly, change is occurring all around you. Apart from the climate, you and others are changing, hopefully for the better, because most of you who read these chapters are on the spiritual path and are gradually raising your consciousness higher as time progresses, through meditation, prayer and spiritual upliftment. This is being given to you from us, the Ascended Masters, and that band of us who are working to help mankind through this transition period.

It is a time of great awareness of the new energies that have been pouring down from heaven to the Earth. That light that you have been bringing down through yourselves, filling and purifying you, and sending it down into the centre of the Earth where light is required. All of you have been helping at this time by bringing these energies and the light through you, and shining your light upon others, helping them to appreciate what can be done through regular meditation, trying to enlighten those who are ready to accept the word of God. Your lives will continue as before, you will still be taking part in your normal activities of various kinds, meeting others either through work or leisure. Those you come into contact with may notice a change in you and perhaps remark on it, or they may have noticed that you have become stronger in your faith or perhaps more confident.

All of this will occur gradually and you may not be aware of it, it may happen almost overnight that you awaken feeling more confident in your faith. It is important that your faith is strong now, ready to impart the wisdom that you have been acquiring both from the teachings and other spiritual books. Those channelled from the Ascended Masters, particularly Alice Bailey, who was intelligent enough to be capable of passing on work by the Master D.K. This is not the type of work that can be read by the 'man in the street', but it is work that has been extremely important to all mankind. Numerous people have read it over the years since it was recorded and translated into other languages, so that throughout the world many have benefited from this work. But I am directing my words to those who are intelligent enough to appreciate these changes, and yet find the work of Alice Bailey and Madame Blavatsky difficult. Madame Blavatsky's work is even more complex, but she was a pioneer in the past for those who were capable of understanding the work that she brought through. Those have read her dramatic book 'The Secret Doctrine' are academically capable of assimilating this work.

My words are simpler, but they have the same meaning and the same purpose for mankind. It is for the upliftment of man's soul, so that the soul from now onwards will not have to suffer more karma in future years. Once the ascension takes place that wheel of rebirth and karma will then cease to turn, and you will find that you have completed your difficult tasks on Earth, and just have to pass on the knowledge that you have gained to those ready to ascend after you.

You will be taking your place in helping both yourselves and others through the work that you will undertake from now on. You will accept the responsibility of your awakening, and awaken others by helping them to ascend with you. Your new life will be one of great importance, and there is so much to be done, so shoulder your responsibilities and accept these words when you feel that you can. Know that there is great love surrounding you and help will be given to you at all times. Ask and you shall receive, knock and the door shall be opened unto you, and that lighted doorway will shine before you and beckon you through into the light when the time comes.

Do not worry if you have not seen that doorway or window waiting for you. It means that it has not been the time for you to approach the threshold yet. All is being taken care of and know that your new life will be awaiting you when you work from both fifth and third dimensions together, helping others through that doorway when they are ready. There will be a time once all are through the doorway when you will wait to return to Earth, when it will be all renewed, peaceful and beautiful once again. The Earth herself will be ready to receive you and make that new life a wonderful one for future days for you and generations who are waiting to take part in that new life with you.

You will be able to see the kingdoms that you cannot at present. Perhaps some of you can see the Devic Kingdoms and others who are in the realms of light occasionally, but once you have passed into that higher dimension, they will be ready to greet you, and many who were lost to you will be found once more, loved ones who will be there to greet you. There is so much to look forward to when all are united and there is no separation any more. There is no true separation, all are one, and all are parts of the whole. It is just that for some time past, man has been separate because he cannot see the unity that is truly his. He is truly part of the one, all that Cosmic Consciousness and the different kingdoms of the Earth that you are unaware of at present. They will be united with you and man will truly come into his own, once more as the being of great power, light and spirituality that he once was.

We from the higher realms greet you and bless you, and we give you our strength and hope, comfort and love for the future.
God bless, Sananda.

As was given in book one, we shall conclude with this simple Invocation to the Light, which is powerful, that asks for Michael the archangel to be present.

> "Wielder of the Sword of Light come forth.
> Defend man from his darkness.
> May God's pure Divine Light shine through the hearts of men,
> And love and peace prevail."

TEACHINGS FROM THE ASCENDED MASTERS

PART FOUR

TEACHINGS FROM THE MASTERS
Book Four

CONTENTS	Page
Section 1 – Master Jesus/Sananda	123
Section 2 – Master Jesus/Sananda	126
Section 3 – Master Jesus/Sananda	128
Section 4 – Master Jesus/Sananda	131
Section 5 – Master Jesus/Sananda	134
Section 6 – Master Jesus/Sananda	137
Section 7 – Master Jesus/Sananda	141
Section 8 – Master Jesus/Sananda	145
Section 9 – Master Jesus/Sananda	149
Section 10 – Master Jesus/Sananda	152
Section 11 – Master Jesus/Sananda	156
Section 12 – Master Jesus/Sananda	159

Channelled by Beryl Charnley

TEACHINGS FROM THE ASCENDED MASTERS-1

I am happy to greet you this day and I hope that we will have many communications for some time. You have been bringing down the violet fire and attempting to spiral it around you as advised. It is not necessary for these details as you have brought down the pure white radiance from the Christ Star, and that is how you should always begin your meditations, and if you wish to bring down the violet fire immediately following the white light, this is good, because then you can concentrate on your meditation. It is too much to expect people to bring down the violet fire later in their meditation because this conflicts with the meditative mood. It matters not when you do this as long as you do it, because it helps to raise the vibratory rate of those who are using it at this time, and also the vibratory rate of the planet at one and the same time. The Earth herself is rising into the fourth dimension, but whatever you do, benefit's the planet too. Pouring down the white light and the violet flame into the heart of the Earth is beneficial.

It takes a little time to get used to these things, but as you gradually use this violet fire from St Germain or Master R, it is helping to clear any negativity around you, and uplift you. Do not worry about the silver ray that is mixed with it now, and do not complicate things by trying to spiral the light around you, this is not essential and it will happen gradually on its own. It is difficult to remember everything. If you have too much to think about you cannot meditate freely. The most important thing is to clear your mind once you have brought down these beams of light, and to try to rise upwards, lifting your consciousness as you did before in that bubble of light if you wish, or if you prefer just go straight upwards as you would in a lift, passing many levels as you do so. This is another method of rising upwards to meet us half way so to speak, into the realms above you.

It is good to imagine this rather than thinking of the God within you, because as a result, although He is within you, you are consciously rising upwards and concentrating on being a part of the spiritual realms, which you are. It is that light body that you must try and concentrate on at present, because it is that part of you that is the most important. It is your spiritual self that has always been there in and around you. Do not be confined to your physical self because that is only a very small part of you, you are within and around, spreading outwards and combining with the auras of those who are with you. This matters not because wherever you are; your aura will mingle with the auras of others. It is only when you conflict with their aura that you find it uncomfortable, but if you find any confliction, try to send forth that violet fire towards them, as well as love, and you will be surprised at the reaction you receive. In time you will find that those people with whom you felt an inner conflict will change in their attitude, and your attitude will change too as a result. You must work at it and try to send forth unconditional love. It is not an easy task, but if you do so, you will find it so much easier to be pleasant and find that they too have a courtesy towards you they did not have before.

All is change at this time. There are many changes occurring both physical and spiritual, and you will find that even if you have no idea what the change will be, for instance, moving house or a job change, any large changes in your life will possibly occur. In some way, each individual will find change occurring for good or bad, but mostly you will find that there will be benefits. Despite not wanting any change you will find that it is for the good and you will be happy with the result. Nothing continues the same way, there is always change around you.

Spiritual change is occurring constantly although you may not be aware of it. I am sure you are aware that more people are turning towards their spirituality, searching for something that has eluded them for some time. Some may not know what they are searching for, but many people particularly in this area of the North who have not previously been on the spiritual path are turning towards it, opening themselves to the reality of it and filled with enthusiasm. We in the spiritual realms are delighted to see this, and have been working towards this end, because previously there has been little interest. Small pockets of individuals have been on the spiritual path, but it has been like a desert here, with no leaders, no real focus, but now there is great interest and there is a light shining from this area, becoming stronger all the time.

You have been bringing down white light, and it is becoming more apparent that increasingly more groups or individuals have been working with the light, and that light is joining with our light becoming one as we all are, and there has been a great move towards this throughout the various northern counties. Scotland too has become a larger centre of light, so we are delighted with the progress that is being made. It is necessary at this time for all of you to become more spiritual in your thoughts, words and deeds, and we expect that throughout the world this new awareness will become more apparent and have a greater impact in shaping humanity's progress into a higher dimension. There are still areas where there is great negativity and violence throughout the world. This has unfortunately always been so, but at this time it is the darkness before the light. The storm that must come to a head before the light can overtake it, which it will.

In working with light you can overcome the forces of darkness, and the violet fire can be shone upon these areas. If you work together in a group, it is important to use this violet fire if at all possible. Shine it around your country, and also use it for the good of all humanity. This is a time for light workers to unite in this work and shine forth the light that will overcome the darkness. The pure white light from the Christ Star and also the violet fire. Both of these lights are necessary at this time, to help both the Earth and humanity, creating a core, a focus to concentrate that desire to uplift the Earth and humanity on to a higher level of being, and erase the negativity and violence in certain areas of the Earth. Use it for the good of all and we, the Masters, will help you with this work. God's blessings be upon you and all who work with you. Sananda.

TEACHINGS FROM THE ASCENDED MASTERS-2

My greetings to you this day, this is Sananda. Have faith and know that I wish to speak about many things regarding humanity at this time. So many are becoming aware of their spirituality. Many who have been unaware up to now are awakening to this reality and learning to meditate, and to listen for that inner voice. It is very simple to do this once the mind is stilled, thoughts dispelled, and that inner peace discovered, all you need to do is to centre yourself and listen for that still small voice. As you know, so many of you who read these words do this each day, and it only needs this word to be spread abroad so that more become aware and are truly part of the spirit world on the physical plane. It is important at this time to recognise the fact that the Earth is gradually rising upwards to a higher dimension, and you yourselves must be ready to accept this.

Forget those men of violence and evil because they will be taken from this Earth when the time comes for the changes to rapidly come about. As you know, those who are ready to move on and upwards will find this a simple task, but those men of violence will be taken into spirit and then reincarnate upon another third dimensional planet of which they know nothing at present, but then they know nothing about their spirituality. They have turned their backs on their task in this lifetime and only want power and cruelty.

We intend to enforce light upon the Earth. It is gradually spreading and will overcome that darkness. What you need to do now is to spread the word so that you can help that light to become so much stronger. Send your light out towards others and you will be surprised at the power of that light. Those who are treading the spiritual path know that the God within is always present, and they can share their problems and pleasures with Him. Always remember that you are never alone, as you know. In bringing down the Christ Light, that pure white radiance to fill you and your homes with light, and pour it down into the centre of the Earth, it helps the Earth increase her ability to rise upwards and cleanse negativity, and in bringing down the violet fire from Saint Germain or Master R, this is an important integral part of the cleansing of humanity and the Earth.

You are ready to spread this word to others now. Remember that it is possible to send this violet flame during healing of others, either directly or otherwise. It is also possible to send this flame to all the violent places and those who are suffering in these areas. Envelop them with the flame and if you can form a vortex over these areas, so much the better, because a vortex is very powerful. You are attempting to put this spiral of violet flame around you when you bring it down, this flame will burn off any negativity around you and those you heal. Healing is also a means of removing negativity from others. The disease that they have is often caused through negative thoughts or lifestyle. It is very easy to succumb to this if you do not have your spirituality at heart. So many neglect this side of themselves and as a result they become ill.

Illness can be caused through thought just as easily as through catching a virus of some kind. In fact a virus can be caught more easily if you are low in spirit. If you are feeling down, then that is often a time when you contract some form of illness. The mind is a powerful tool and if you use it for the good of yourselves and others, then you can overcome many illnesses, and things that you would not imagine possible. Direct your thoughts always towards positivity, light and love, and you will be amazed at how powerful this can be.

The Great Invocation was given at a time when the power of light was necessary for the world. It has always been so because mankind needs to overcome his darkness, but use the Invocation daily and use the words very powerfully and you will help the Earth to overcome all negativity and evil. Say the words with meaning out loud, and even more power is created when said in a group. As you know a group can be extremely powerful, and centre light within it to be sent out for the Earth's benefit and all humanity.

Whenever two or three are gathered together in my name, there I am in the midst of you. Know this and know that my love flows out towards you. Use this love to link you together, and to send this love and light, using it as a powerful tool to direct light towards others who are in need of this. Think well of where you wish to send it, and direct it forcefully. I will guide you. Ask and it shall be given unto you, and you the seekers will find what you are searching for, and this life will be one of service and redemption. May God's blessings be upon you and all who work with you.
Sananda.

TEACHINGS FROM THE ASCENDED MASTERS-3

My greetings to you this day. This is Sananda, and I wish to speak on many things over the course of time. All of you who read these words are presently working on the white light and violet fire. Both of these will be helping you to rise upwards to the higher dimensions, which are required by all light workers at this time. Throughout the world there are many thousands doing this work, and as a result there is a network filled with light across the world, who link with the realms of light, channelling this light to the many places throughout the world that need it. Both to places where there is violence, and to people who need help from their suffering. Healing light is pouring down from above to help them, and from you across the world as you use that light as a tool, and the violet fire is proving to be quite powerful in this way, to burn away any negativity that has been produced by those men of violence.

In time there will be a great change throughout humanity, a change for the better. The light is overcoming the darkness. We can see from the realms above what is occurring, we can see the whole picture whereas you see only a tiny part. It is like your lives, you cannot see the whole but we can, and is like a jigsaw puzzle of which you can only see one portion. There are many ways of seeing everything, many dimensions into the whole, and as you can only see a small portion of the picture that the jigsaw is making, you cannot know what the whole picture is until the time comes when it is revealed unto you. When you rise into the fifth dimension then you can get the whole picture, it is at that time that your lives will be truly fulfilled. All of you are working towards this now, gradually rising upwards to a new level of consciousness you have not reached before. You have not been working on this violet fire of light for long, but it is gradually gathering momentum, and even though you feel no different, there is a difference in the atmosphere around and within you, that ether is becoming finer. Your bodies will be creating a new finer body that will come to pass in time. You will be more amorphous eventually, and be able to recreate your bodies in the new dimension of light.

As time goes by, mankind will help to create this new Earth that is going to change your ways of living. As the Earth herself rises into this new dimension, she will create new horizons, new ways in which man will have to live to keep up with the Earth herself. She is rising upwards ahead of you, and unless you change with her, then humanity will be left behind. It is only those who are light workers and others who live good lives, who will be able to rise into this new dimension, those who already live their lives to the full in the best way possible, helping others, but unaware of their true spirituality. You and those people who I have just described will be able to cope with the changes around you, and you will be able to help them through this transition stage.

All will be revealed to you, and the ways of men will alter. Life will take on a richer, fuller meaning because the link with us in the realms above will be constant. You will no longer have to sit quietly to meditate in order to link with your guides and the God within. You will be able to link with us as a matter of course, and be able to live physically, and link spiritually at one and the same time. This was done in the past when men and God were one, and now this will come about once more. It is a time of great rejoicing, a time that God has waited for, for so long. Mankind is choosing to go along the spiritual path, to make that full change and to rise into his new capabilities. The time of awakening is now, and more are learning to appreciate what capabilities they have within them. The whole wisdom of the world is within each one of you if you learn how to tap into that Universal Mind. What is life all about if you cannot be aware of your full potential? It is a time when man will come into his own; it is a time that he has been waiting for, for so long.

Many of you have felt that you wished to know the reason why, to receive the answer to many unanswered questions in your minds. What is life about? Why are we here? There must be more to life than just living in a constant routine that you can never change. The life that you will live is something that is beyond comprehension. It is something that you have been searching for, hoping to have revealed to you. You may wish that you could change the way you live, to make it more worthwhile, to redeem yourselves and to be able to face up to any challenges that are given to you. Many people face challenges such as mountaineering, always striving to reach the highest peak, some have given their lives for this, just to be able to do something that no one has ever done before. These great challenges, physical, mental and spiritual, are given to all at some time, and some meet them head on. Others will avoid meeting this challenge, but I know that most of you who are on the spiritual path wish to know the answers to many questions about life and its purpose.

The time has come when all will be revealed to you once you have reached that transition stage, and it is upon you now. Your answers will be given at this time. Answers to all these questions about life and the realms of light beyond to which you return at the end of each incarnation, and keep on returning as each lifetime goes by, but this life that you are living at present may be the last one which you need to incarnate. You will be constantly part of the realms of light and life on Earth together from now on. Once you have reached the fifth dimension, you need never pass that transition any more. Life will be eternal as it was meant to be, and you will continue rising up through the dimensions, but without passing away at the end of the lifetime, dying as you call it, and you will learn many things that have never been revealed before to mankind. All you have to do is work with the light, filling yourselves and the Earth with the white and violet light.

Continue with this work and as time goes by you will find many truths given to you.

I, Sananda, and all who work with me will guide you, and if you wish for help in any way, ask and it will be given unto you, you only need to ask. All is very well. God bless and keep you all.
Sananda.

TEACHINGS FROM THE ASCENDED MASTERS-4

My greetings to you all this day, all workers for light. I give you grateful thanks for all that you have been doing in bringing down both the white and violet light into the Earth, and spreading it across the whole world. This light is prevailing and pervading the darkness, that negativity that is gradually lessening. You may not realise because of all the violence, and the bad news that you hear on television and radio, but as you always say, good news is not news, so it always seems to be negative, but gradually and imperceptibly, the light is prevailing, and we are winning.

There is a great network of beings, beings of light from the realms above who are joining with you in this work. You are never alone, and you know that light workers throughout the whole of the world are really beginning to make their mark. It is a time of triumph because the darkness is receding. Always there has been negativity, ever since the world began; there are always the two opposites. It would not be normal if there were not the two extremes, but recently the tremendous amount of violence and evil is beginning to disappear, and now we, from the realms of light, are able to see what is being done.

When you are upon the physical plane you can only see in three dimensions, but in time you will be able to see much more, almost as much as we can. At present that little part of the picture is all you see, what you see around you and what you hear about, but in time once you have reached that higher dimension of light, there are so many things you will know about instantly, and be able to take part in much more than you are doing presently. Even though you are working with light, once you have accessed that higher dimension, there will be much more scope for you if you have the will to do the work that is required of you. All light workers have chosen this path; you chose it before you incarnated in this lifetime. As you know, once you have passed through into the physical, your memories of what you chose to do are lost unless you have the capability of tapping that Universal Mind to know everything. That time will come, but normally once you have chosen your path, you accept that, and hope that once you have become adult, you will hold onto that spiritual path and do the work you chose.

You have some doubts at times, and as I have said before, many of you have asked why? What are you here for? What is the meaning of life? You have minds to think, and free will to choose, and sometimes the wrong path is chosen. You have forgotten what it was you chose to do, but this is only human, and humanity has free will. He has a choice of what he will do in his life; we hope that those who forgot will remember before the end of their incarnation. Now is a time of change, and now is a time of awakening, it is a time when many of you chose to be a part of this awakening, to help those who are struggling and beginning to question the church's teachings. There are many religions of course, but sometimes these religions can be rather blinkered in their outlook, not realising the freedom there is in choosing this spiritual path. It is not necessary for many trappings of splendour in churches and those who preach in them, some of them have become more splendid over the years and it is quite unessential.

If you look back to the life that I as Jesus led, it was one of simplicity and austerity, and yet towards the end of my life there was a multitude who followed me and my disciples, and we did not have these splendid trappings that are within some of the churches that exist today. It is a matter of choice of course, but sometimes those who preach are led astray, and do not realise that they have taken upon themselves the practice of splendour rather than that of austerity. They have almost become little gods themselves, and have fettered humanity with those trappings, and the outlook that is within those temples of worship has become changed over the years. I do not wish to decry any religion because all who worship mean well, and those who preach to them mean well. It is only that sometimes they do not allow the worshippers any freedom in their outlook.

I hope that all of you who read these words have your own idea of praising God, and I leave it to you to choose the way that you feel is right for you. This is what I mean by the freedom of choice, because nowadays there is a more informal approach, and I hope that you will choose this rather than the splendour that is prevailing in some of the churches. I myself, feel that whatever feels right in your heart is what is right for you, do not accept anything that does not feel correct, and do not believe everything you hear. Question it in your hearts, and once you feel that this is right; then you must adhere to that faith and follow it truly. That is all that I wish for anyone, the truth, because you must have faith, true faith in everything, otherwise you cannot believe sincerely in confidence. Confidence comes through trust, and I know that you have trust in all that I have been speaking about over the months and years that I have been channelling these thoughts.

The future of humanity is bright. There is so much to look forward to, so much to believe in, knowing that power will come to you. The light and love that is emanating from the realms above towards you, is from the Masters and God, the source of all being. This is what He chose for mankind, knowing that in time, man with his free will would move upwards and become a true being of light, working for the Creator and becoming one with Him, as man always was and always should be. It was only when the fall of man came, that humanity became separated from the one true God, and felt that he must keep worshipping from afar rather than being a part of Him, which you are, all of you. That divinity is within you and it just needs rekindling for mankind to come into his own.

We have faith in you if you will have faith in us, and remember that through meditation and upliftment of the consciousness, you can become a true being of light, rising to that higher vibration, that higher dimension of being that is truly yours for the asking. In time to come, there will be many changes, they have been occurring for some time, imperceptibly, but they are gradually gaining momentum, and the changes that will come about through the Earth will, we hope, be gentle and peaceful. It is up to humanity to reach up to that higher state of being, and keep up with the Earth as she also rises up to that higher dimension.

It is only necessary to have faith enabling you to work with us, the Masters of the Hierarchy. I, Sananda, am working with many beings of light, as I have said, with Michael, and many beings from other planets who have been communicating with the Earth for some time. We have united and are collaborating with one another. The channel who is working with me has heard from several beings of light who live on other planets, but have been travelling about the Earth for some time helping when they can, and are ready for the time of change. We have said that this time of change will come about within several years. It is always difficult to predict exactly when things will happen in earthly terms, because, as you know, time does not exist here but is man made, and therefore all depends on the level which humanity reaches within those few years. If light workers continue to prevail against the darkness, and we ourselves help as we have been doing over the centuries, more so in recent years, then that time will be less.

Everything depends on man's attitude to others, but love will prevail. Light will prevail against the darkness, and I promise you that whatever happens, you will be under our protective care, and the new life that will come about will be one that is a new awakening. New horizons beckon, and that life to come will be truly worth living for all of you. God bless and keep you all.
Sananda.

TEACHINGS FROM THE ASCENDED MASTERS-5

My greetings to you this day, this is Sananda. There is so much to say that it is difficult to know where to begin. You have read an address given by a retired Lt. Colonel in the United States Air force where he gives accounts of U.F.O.'s and Extra Terrestrials over the many years that he served. All this has occurred and has been kept quiet by the governments of the world, it is the truth and it has been the truth over the centuries. It was revealed that all these U.F.O.'s could travel across the dimensions, and many could travel through time, and I am sure that you have realised this before now, and recognised the fact that it happened in Biblical times and before that. The Bible has referred many times to objects that were indescribable and unbelievable to those simple men, and when you think about it, as you have before you have wondered whether it might have been some kind of spaceship, and of course it was. Many times this has occurred, and certain descriptions in the Bible refer to beings that have arrived from a spacecraft, and as a result that being has been revered and referred to as a God. All this has happened many times, and in places scattered throughout the world.

Over the centuries, these occurrences have been accepted in different ways, in more recent years, as they truly are, other beings from worlds unseen to you. They have come from afar to view this planet, and to help those upon it over the millennia. As you have been told, I have come from another planet also. I was from Venus, and when I came to Earth as Jesus and was born to Mary, there was a spacecraft, a large one that slowly moved across the skies, and which in those days was referred to as a star. It looked like a brilliant star, and the three wise men followed that star, but it was told in a different way, because they were aware, at least one of them was aware of astronomy and many other things. Arcane knowledge he knew, and was aware that it would not be a star, and that it was more likely to be a spacecraft. They had more knowledge than the other simple men who wrote these accounts in the Bible, and they were aware that this craft was hovering over Bethlehem. That craft came from Venus. Other craft were there to see what was occurring, this important event in the history of men, because as you know, many spacecraft can be cloaked, and are not seen as a result, and at that time no knowledge of my identity was given to anyone apart from the wise men.

In future times there were other beings who were deified or revered such as Buddha, Krishna, Allah and Zarathustra, all these were looked upon as great Gods, and of course they did much good. They were a part of religious history, and are still revered. Buddha came from Venus too, he too has been referred to as a great being, and he truly lived a good life. He rejected all the riches that he had, and like many others, he had come from another planet like myself, and known a different way of life. He had the capability of doing things that other men could not do, causing miracles to occur, and as a result, those who worshipped him imagined that he was a god. It was understandable that men worshipped beings who appeared to be able to create miracles, and who appeared as though they had bodies of light. This effect of course is because we lived in another dimension, and were able to bring that ability with us when we came upon the Earth, to create miracles and cause strange things to occur that were unbelievable to those around us, always for the good of men, and always so that mankind would believe in God, whichever god it was they turned to.

Each being which has been revered in the religions of the world has come for that reason, to help man to look up to God and to believe in Him because He always has been, and always will be the God of all, the Creator of all things. Over the centuries He has caused mankind to believe in many things through the introduction of these beings from other worlds. They have come to help man and will continue to do so. Many civilisations have been built through these beings from other worlds. The Aztecs and the Incas were two civilisations that have mythical legends going back over the centuries. Quetzalcoatl was one who was referred to by the Aztecs, who wore a feathered cloak that was symbolic, and he came from another planet, and brought about that new civilisation. Pyramids were built and many myths have been handed down over the centuries, some of them rather bloodthirsty, but on the whole, most of the legends are true. The Egyptian civilisations have been based from the days of Atlantis, where again, there were pyramids, and the Egyptian ones were based on those Atlantean pyramids. There were beings from Sirius who helped at this time, and have helped over the ages, being very advanced compared with mankind.

As you can imagine, if you will allow your minds to open a little more, you can then accept the fact that they came from the future as well as from space, and that certain buildings and civilisations came about as a result of these space people, or extra terrestrials as they are called. They have evolved to a very high degree, and their knowledge is surpassing everything known to man, even now. If you reckon that mankind has learnt a great deal technologically over the last twenty years, then consider that these beings have known all that for hundreds of years and expanded on it, and you can realised how much more they have stored away in their minds and on their planets, and recognise how very lowly man's knowledge is compared with theirs. There is nothing wrong with this, it is just that they are so much more advanced, light years ahead in other words, most of them, compared with humanity. Comparisons are odious I know, but this is just to give you an idea of how evolved they are.

I have been working with a great number of these extra terrestrials over the years, and we are working together for the good of all, this includes those upon the Earth, who are attempting to raise upwards and join with them, so that all of you are a part of the true Cosmic Civilisation spreading out into the galaxies and uniting with all beings who are upon the fifth and sixth dimensions. It matters not at present where you are, but we know that you are attempting to raise your consciousness and your awareness on to higher levels as time goes by, accepting many things that will occur once you have crossed the threshold of higher dimensions. All of you light workers are attempting to understand and accept what we are presenting to you. We know that it is difficult to realise how much more you have to learn in order to be a part of God's Plan. You were given free will to do whatever you wished, to evolve or not, and all of you who read these words have accepted the challenge to evolve your souls to a higher level. Love is an important part of that plan that you accept, unconditional love for all, and is part of your inheritance. We hope that you will continue to try to use this love and extend your hearts to all beings of light, either on the Earth or in the realms above within space. Do not let there be a barrier between yourselves and others who dwell within the Universe.

Over the centuries, many civilisations have come and gone, but they have been started by extra terrestrials who united with humanity on Earth, and helped mankind to raise the standard of their lives, so that many were given true knowledge over the centuries that otherwise would have been lost. Given extra abilities such as psychic, telepathic and other abilities that had not been known upon the Earth before, and over those years, mankind has improved his lot as a result. It is sometimes difficult to accept these things but it is the truth and over the next few communications I will help you to understand these things, and to help you to appreciate what has occurred in the past, and what will occur in the future for man. As I have said before, there is much to look forward to, and your knowledge, your capabilities will improve, and are improving more quickly as the years go by.

Think on these things, believe them and know that I would not lead you astray. I had to wait until you accepted this from another. It would not have been right for you to have heard these truths from me to begin with; it would have appeared as heresy, and I would not wish this to happen. All of you must continue to believe in God the Source of all being, and know that He will never forsake you, and neither will I. God bless and keep you all.
Sananda.

TEACHINGS FROM THE ASCENDED MASTERS-6

I give you my greetings this day, this is Sananda. I know that you are still assimilating the most recent communications that have knocked aside the cornerstone of all religions. I hope you may accept this, but I think that most of you still have that true faith in God, and in We the Masters of the Hierarchy. The God who is the Source, who created everything, everything that you know that exists, from time immemorial, those stars and planets that you see in the night sky, that have twinkled there over the millennia. They have changed obviously as time has progressed, their position has altered, but nevertheless, their existence has been created by Him, that Great Being who has existed always, the Source of everything that is and ever will be. You have within you a part of that Being, that true divinity that is at the core of every living creature on each planet and star throughout the universes, and therefore this tiny golden spark within you is the link that is necessary, and gives you the confidence to know all beings belong to God.

You are all part of the whole, we all have God's divine spark within us, understand that you are never separate from God, and that is all that is necessary to know. When you are aware of this, then you will have the faith to continue without the complete Bible story as the basis of the Christian belief. It matters not that the star that was believed in from the beginning was not a star, but a spacecraft. The true heart of Christianity is the actual story of the birth of myself as Jesus, and also the other religions involved have at their heart a being, a great being of light, and this is true. All these religions are based on a being, a man who was good and who caused miracles to occur. Everything is true, it is just that each one of us has come from another planet, is an evolved soul, and therefore the religions are based on truth and goodness, therefore there can be no harm in them. Those whom you worship, those who were worshipped in the past truly deserved to be revered in some way, looked up to, and their lives emulated by those who attempted to be like them, which was good, and we hope that this will continue over the years to come.

You have all taken part in many lifetimes, and have been gradually evolving your souls to a higher level, towards an awakening to new ideals and principles. Each one of you has had the capability of doing many things in the past that you may not always remember.

The lives that you lived are remembered by your higher self, that part of you that has incarnated each time, but the lower self, your physical being, is not aware of what has taken place in past lives unless you have the capability of being able to tap into your higher self to discover these capabilities of which you were able. But this is not important as it is now that matters, not the past but the future, and you are destined for great things in this lifetime. There are plans for mankind to rise and be creators of their own destiny. Humanity is gradually drawing towards a higher level of being, into the fifth dimension, and above in future days, but now is the time when you are preparing for this, and we know that you are all attempting to raise your consciousness onto that level where you can hear our thoughts, the thoughts of those who are important in their communications with mankind. The Masters and myself, the Angelic beings who help me and who serve God, and the God within you, the I Am presence, are all helping to uplift you and to pass on knowledge that is essential for your future wellbeing, and for the wellbeing of those who are not yet aware of us, or cannot yet receive our communications. They are the ones who are stumbling towards the path of truth, a spiritual path on which you walk, and are attempting to help those who are ready to receive these words.

In the past few decades there have been researchers into the truth, who have written books that have stimulated interest in extra terrestrials, and the possibility of spacecraft looking down upon the Earth, and landing in various places. Erich Von Daniken wrote several books in which he had researched knowledge, that those of you who read these books have in your subconscious. He explained how there are various places in the Earth where obviously men from outer space have been represented on paintings and carvings. Many of these places are out of reach for most of you, in Peru, and on islands that few of you can visit. These places have been depicted in his books. There have been areas in mountainous regions through which tunnels have been excavated, tunnels that bear no resemblance to normal ones created by mankind. They are smooth and disappear many hundreds of feet into the heart of the mountains, and have obviously been created by people who have an ability to cut through solid rock without leaving marks of machines or tools. It is still a mystery to mankind as to how they were made, but obviously there was a capability that has not yet been passed on.

Many mysteries have been written about over the past few decades, and I know that some of you are extremely interested in this, and have tried to find out more. Always searching in a quest for wisdom, and it is good to have an enquiring mind, an open mind to realities that could conceivably be true, and most of which are true. At one time civilisations existed in these areas that have been lost over the centuries, and these civilisations have originated by beings from other planets. It is perfectly possible for this to happen without the general public being aware, and over the centuries past, these civilisations existed on their own in these remote areas, attempting to leave behind some mark to show that they had lived on your planet without causing any problems to those around them. They created many beautiful monuments that were left and have been covered by forest and undergrowth.

This has been cleared in some areas in order that those who have been able to visit them can see these statues and pyramids. It is only those with the time and capability to explore these places, those of an adventurous spirit, and who can afford to explore these areas, so that they could carry back the knowledge to others who otherwise would never have known about it.

Those who have lived on the Earth, having landed from other planets and stars have been benevolent and wish no harm to anyone living here. They have only tried to do good, and to create new civilisations as I mentioned in my previous communication. The Aztecs and Incas are those I had in mind who have attempted to help humanity, and to change the area so that it was possible to live comfortably, in a place that might otherwise have been a problem with the high altitude. The land around them was cultivated in terraces on the high ground, and buildings created in places that might otherwise have not been considered habitable. I know that many of these places are inaccessible to most humans because of their remoteness, but many beings of light have been able to visit them. Masters, and other beings meet together, and unite in thought with others who have been unable to reach those areas, but have meditated in caverns or houses below, linking their minds with those above them, and learning many truths.

In this way, communications have been channelled to those who have been receptive to these thoughts, and many beings from stars far away such as Arcturus, the Pleiades, Sirius and Orion, so many that they are countless, but all these beings have attempted to communicate with us, those on Earth, and those Masters of the Hierarchy. All are working together for the good of mankind, and in time to come, humanity will be joining us on that higher dimension, the fifth, to which the Earth herself is rising. You, and others like you are part of the vanguard to help mankind at this time of change. That is your task at this time, to try to change the attitude of those with closed minds, to try to enlighten them in some way, and help our inspiration to come to them also. So many people are wrapped up in their own lifestyle and do not wish to know anything about the future or about these things on which I have been talking. The fact that others are all around, beings from other planets have been walking upon the Earth over the centuries from time to time, and have not been noticed by anyone unless they have eyes to see.

Many are able to adapt themselves to a new lifestyle, and there are others who have been unseen in the crafts above the planet, and projected down onto your planet with you, but as they are on another dimension, you must realise that you cannot see them. They have been mingling with you over the centuries, and as with spiritual guidance, attempting to pass on their knowledge, their wisdom and inspiration to mankind. Like ourselves, they work telepathically, and have helped those who have been working on technology over the past thirty or forty years, and as a result, there have been new innovations made, which have not necessarily come from those who have been working on them, but inspired by others unseen. Reflect on this and realise that this is perfectly possible, when you think about the third dimension compared with the fifth, and realise that you can be accompanied constantly by anyone from the fifth dimension, and of course by those unseen helpers, the Angelic Hierarchy and the Masters of whom we have spoken constantly. All these things can be dwelt upon, and your minds expanded to accept them, and then to recognise that all this is true, and that the future is bright for all of you. Think on these things, and open your minds to new horizons, and accept what is the truth.

As time progresses, more wisdom will be given to you, and you will be able to gradually accept these new awakened thoughts.
I give you my blessing this day, to all of you. God bless.
Sananda.

TEACHINGS FROM THE ASCENDED MASTERS-7

My greetings to you this day, to those who read these words. I hope that these communications are of interest to all. I know that perhaps there have been some changes in your attitude towards the religion that you have believed in from early days, it takes some time to adjust your belief and still have faith in the basis of your religion. We do not wish to shatter your faith because it is most important that you hang on to this belief, it is still early days and I know that all of you who tread the spiritual path accept that change is all around you. There are changes in everything that you see; the whole structure of human life has been changing over the past decades. Everything is ready; all is prepared for the change that will be most important to you all. We have arranged everything, but it is up to you to make the final change in your living style, that change that you are aware of to raise your consciousness sufficiently, to move upwards, ever upwards into higher dimensions of living.

We have been preparing you gradually, and hope that you are ready to accept this now. You have read about this in books that have been channelled, and also you have been told by myself and others, who have been sending forth our thoughts to all who channel them, to inform you that everything is about to take place when ready. I know it is difficult to take that final step, and there must be time given for you to practice raising your consciousness and lifting sufficiently high enough in order that you can see that threshold of light through which you should pass. Some see it as a lighted doorway that is inviting you to step through; others see it as a lighted stairway into the realms of light. All is symbolic, but all is ready for you to step into that realm of light, onto the fourth dimension, and eventually the fifth. We have been waiting for you to take that step into the unknown. It is a difficult time perhaps, but this is a time of great change, and I know that you have the faith to accept this as the truth, which it is, but it does take a little time, and you must have patience, and just acknowledge that you will cross that threshold when the time is right for you.

Some have already done so, and have found that they can work perfectly adequately within the two dimensions, and they have a new perception of life, an expectation that has never been known before, apart from those beings who are Avatars, and who constantly cross that threshold while they are creating miracles. Existing in two places at once, such as Sai Baba, who holds court when he holds his darshan, and yet he can be right across the world helping others in a situation that might otherwise have been disastrous for them. This is achieved through working on the fifth dimension, and being upon the third simultaneously. You have much work to do before you are able to achieve this capability, but as time progresses this will be possible for you all. You only need faith to take that step onto the fourth dimension initially.

Those of us who are working with humanity at this time are giving you our support, and all the help that is necessary to achieve this result. As I said before, it is a time of great change for all of you, particularly those of you in the vanguard who are taking those first timorous steps across the threshold of light. Be not afraid, have faith and as we have always said, say a prayer or invocation before reaching your consciousness as high as you possibly can. This is the most important part, to separate yourselves from your normal mundane life and thoughts, and be in a place where you will be uninterrupted at this time. I know it is difficult for some of you to do this, but I know that you will be capable of it very soon. You will have been practicing raising your consciousness by visualising rising upwards in a lift to many floors above you, perhaps the ninth or tenth floor, and in this way you can raise your consciousness quite easily and quickly, so that you yourself are left sitting and your consciousness is way above you in the spiritual realms. This is the simplest way of rising upwards towards your guide or whoever is directing you, perhaps the I AM presence or higher self, it all depends who you feel most comfortable with. Just have faith and know that all will be well. You are protected always when you pray, and your guide or Guardian Angel will be with you at all times.

Much of humanity is on the brink of accepting what you have known for some years. These people live good lives and are faithful to their religion, but perhaps need a little help adjusting at this time of change, and I know that you are aware that this is part of your work as service to humanity and God. Part of your future work, to help them through this time of change and to drop a word here or there to make them rethink their beliefs, and how they will live in the future. It is difficult sometimes to persuade them. You must not press your way of thought upon them, but if you plant a seed in their minds, they will come back to you when they are ready. You can then explain your way of thinking, and the New Age way of spirituality that we are continuing with into the future, way into the future, and the new dimension in which you will live.

Beings on other planets are aware and have been helping, as you know, from civilisations that they have existed in for so long. They are evolved and have capabilities of which you will soon become aware, and you too will have these capabilities in time. All of us are working towards the end of helping humanity through this great change, and bringing them through into a new way of living, to cross that threshold that will mean so much to you in the future.

Your lives will change dramatically for the better, and you will be able to travel instantly through thought once you have achieved the fifth dimension. It will be gradual, but it is a time when clarity of vision is necessary, that clear capability of achieving this new consciousness. Once you have cleared your mind, so that you can receive our thoughts, you will find it so much simpler to join us on that new dimension and new vibration, and you will be finely tuned by this time to that new level on which we live.

Technically speaking, we live on a vibratory level that is much higher than your own, for instance, television and radio wave lengths very tremendously from your own, and you could not hear or see either until you switch them on. They are above your wavelength of hearing, rather like a dog's whistle that you cannot hear because it is on such a high finely tuned vibration or wavelength. You just have to have the faith to know that it is there, and you know that when you switch on a radio or television that a picture or sound will come. This is exactly the same, except that you cannot see or hear anything until you tune yourself into that wavelength, and then you will hear and eventually see what it is you are striving for. It is a matter of faith, and knowing that we speak the truth, and that humanity is gradually rising upwards with the Earth herself, onto this new level of being.

You just have to take that new turning; you have come to the crossroads in your life when you decide whether to go ahead or not. It is all up to you, but once you have achieved this thought, it is difficult to turn back. You have been given this capability by God, this blessing that you can accept or reject, but why take second best when the best is being given to you? Remember that I, Sananda, work only with the best because I work for God, I always have done, as do those who work with me, the Angels and Archangels, and those of Ashtar Command, from other planets. We have been serving God and helping humanity over the last few decades, all of us are attempting to come together and bring you together through this threshold into a new age, a new Golden Age of life. This is a great achievement, and much work has gone into this, and I know that you and all who work with you are attempting to go with us and achieve this new capability.

Your families and friends will also move upwards, in time, and I know that you will wish this to occur, particularly those of your family who are not yet aware. Do not concern yourselves with them because all will be well, they will receive protection and care at this time of change. You can help them, and you will do once you have achieved this new capability. It will come in due course. Do not worry if it does not happen within the next few weeks, do not pin yourselves down to time, because time does not exist in our dimension. Just remember that truth will prevail, and God will help you through this time of change. Have faith and believe. Accept whatever you can to help you, and I know that you will come through this time with flying colours. Know that we are always with you to help. Ask for help and support, and you will receive it, and know that the time is nigh.

These are exciting days for those who truly believe, and I know that you will do whatever you can to help and encourage those who are not sure. Take your time and know that help is always at hand.

I, Sananda give you God's blessing this day and always. Farewell for now.
Sananda.

TEACHINGS FROM THE ASCENDED MASTERS-8

I, Sananda greet you all this day, and I wish to speak on many things. There will be momentous happenings in the near future, events that you will look forward to with great excitement. I cannot tell you all the details of these happenings because so much depends on the nature of mankind, whether he is ready to accept everything that will change in his life. There are still many who are filled with violence, and their capability of accepting their spirituality is virtually nil, but they are not the ones of whom I wish to speak. I wish to give you hope for the future, that the majority of men and women on this Earth are of good intention, and they are the ones I speak about. You and others who work with the light are ready to accept whatever occurs.

You have been told that changes will come and you are ready and able to accept this. The changes are all for the good, and are gradually occurring as you know. There is a subtle difference in the atmosphere, this has been changing recently, and I think that some of you are aware of this. Maybe few people can see any difference in this, and think that perhaps those who can are imagining it, but gradually and imperceptibly the Earth and yourselves are moving onto a higher plane of existence, and before too long you will have reached that fourth dimension of which I have spoken many times.

The momentous happenings of which I spoke will occur once you have reached this level of existence, and then you will be able to see the devas and little people which a few can see clairvoyantly, and know what they look like. You will find that your eyes will be opened to so many things that are at present invisible to you all. You will be able to see when the climate is about to change, there will be a barrier raised within the sky, so the clouds will appear different to you. You will be able to see when the onset of rain is about to take place before it happens. It sounds rather trivial, but your eyes will be able to take on a new ability, seeing mystical happenings that although apparent to some now, all of you who have reached that new level of existence will manage to see things that are strange to you, but which will be quite normal in the future. You will be able to see some of your loved ones who can come through to visit you when you feel that you can accept this, and I am sure that most of you will be delighted at this. It is something that you must be ready to accept before it happens. They would not wish to alarm you, but you will be able to see and communicate with them. Something that up to now only clairvoyants have been able to do, and I know that you will all accept this in time.

What I mentioned about the climate changes is something that people cannot fully see at present, they can only be guided by meteorologists, who obviously cannot see this happening, but can judge by wind speed, etc., to forecast when the changes will come about. You will be able to look up into the heavens, and for instance, see a storm approaching long before it actually occurs, and you will be ready for this. It is something that animals can sense, but not necessarily see. They can sense the change before it occurs. It is something you may have noticed and realised afterwards, that the animals and birds have taken shelter before the storm occurred. They knew it was going to happen and you will know this in time, and you will also know before good weather occurs. Before a change in temperature is about to take place, there are subtle changes in the sky that you will be able to see; all this is possible in the future. It may not seem important, but they are new capabilities that you will have.

Other things you will be able to see are Angels. At present, I have spoken only of the little people and devas, but the Angelic Hierarchy is part of the devic kingdom. The devas that I mentioned are those who look after the areas in which you live, the large devas, and of course the smaller ones who are in charge of the plants and trees, those you will see too. However, the Angels who protect you and serve God are those of a higher status than the Landscape Angels as you might call them. You will be able to see some of them from time to time, also the healing and ministering Angels who will come and help when you give healing. They are there present and available to all. You may ask for their help and feel that there is someone there helping you and bringing down the healing light from above, but in time to come you will occasionally be able to see them, and I know that it is something to which you look forward, to be able to see all these beings of light.

You will, in time, be able to see your guide, and sometimes your guardian Angel, who protects you individually. Some of you have communicated over the years and only tried to imagine what they are like, but this is for the future. These momentous happenings will occur once you have reached that higher dimension, but in the meantime, I know that you are trying to raise your consciousness ever higher, so that when the time comes, it will be easier for you to make that subtle change. It will occur in the twinkling of an eye, without any undue strenuous effort on your part, when the time is right it will occur and not before. In my last communication, I suggested that you might attempt to reach upwards onto that dimension in your meditations, and I am sure that most of you are attempting to continually reach up and into that higher level of being.

It is those who are unaware of their spirituality that I hope you will attempt to at least plant a seed of awareness in their minds, and they are the ones who we hope will change their attitude towards one of meditation. As we have said in the past, western civilisation normally does not include meditation in their worship. It has always been prayer and hymns of praise to God, which is good, but eastern religion has always included meditation and quiet. I know that during prayer the western religions are quiet, but they are not listening for that inner voice, the voice of God who will speak to them from the centre of their being, in the peace and silence. That is what is required of them, that listening through the inner ear for that still small voice. All of you who read these words have known this for some time, some of you for very many years, but try to pass on this knowledge to those who you know do not meditate, and try to give them the idea that it would do them good. It always brings a peace and stillness to the soul. It cannot do harm, it can only do good, particularly for those who are restless or nervous in any way. The stillness will help them, and if they can completely cast away all their thoughts and just listen and BE, then they will benefit in many ways.

So much of western society now seems to be enveloped in noise. Traffic noise, so-called music in shops and wherever people are sitting, they seem to need noise around them, radios blaring and televisions on, even when the people are not really listening or watching. This seems to be the norm for people, to always have noise around them instead of quiet, particularly when they are at leisure, some need to have this around them. It is difficult to try to change their ways when they have this different attitude, but I know that eventually they will come to accept that at times it is good to be quiet. It is good for the soul and for their spirituality that is there within them, if they will only allow it to come to the surface more and not suppress it.

There are many youngsters who are coming into the world, who are aware of their spirituality, who are aware that they have lived in the past many times. They accept this, and you would be surprised at their knowledge, they are old souls who have come to live at this time on the Earth, and who will guide others in the future once they have become adult. I think some of you may have already discovered this in speaking to children, and perhaps hearing them talking to one another. You will find that in the future there will be a new generation of humanity who will have their divinity closer to the surface, and who will be ready to accept all these changes that are coming to pass very soon. Their attitude of mind will help their parents, who may not be so aware of their spirituality. Many people learn from their children in various ways, in their attitude of mind and the inner knowledge or in the ways that they act.

For instance, it may be that the parents have always eaten meat, and do not wish to vary their diet, as they get older. Perhaps they have not thought deeply about it, about the suffering of animals, and the unnecessary killing of all these creatures for their benefit, but sometimes the children will teach them by example. They have a different way of thinking, and realise that they can eat other products that will benefit them in their diet without eating animal flesh, without having those animals killed for their food. So it will be in the future, that once again all men will live without meat and will eat only the fruits of the Earth, the natural products that can be their diet, and they can live perfectly well without killing animals for food. It was this way when man first lived upon the Earth, and it will be in the future.

All these happenings will occur in due course, this I promise. I know that you hope that all will be well, and I know that you have faith in us, the Masters of the Hierarchy and Angelic Hierarchy, and all who protect and guide you. Our ways are not your ways, but in the future, you will learn how it is that we exist between the two realms, that of light and your physical existence on Earth. We understand you because we have lived upon the Earth also, and we have mastered everything necessary in all the lifetimes we have lived, but we wish to raise you so that you will be enabled to join us on that higher plane of existence without problem, and we will protect and guide you through these changes over the next period of time in which the changes occur. I, Sananda, promise this and wish you well. God bless and keep you always.
Sananda.

TEACHINGS FROM THE ASCENDED MASTERS-9

This is Master R my child. I have not spoken for some time through you, but at this time of change I have been received through many people throughout the world as Saint Germain. As you know, we are one and the same being, and have been attempting to spread the word about using the violet fire of light. This is a powerful light that has been projected downwards from myself to the Earth to burn away any negative thoughts, fears and ignorance from those who are attempting to use their light, the Christ light, so that both colours can integrate together and be used for the good of humanity. This light is extremely powerful and as you know, has great healing within it. You have been attempting to use this light recently, all of you who ready these words, and I know that sometimes it is difficult for you to visualise using it in combination with the white light. It is difficult sometimes to see it swirling around and pouring down into the Earth, but it matters not if you can see it, so long as you try to visualise it pouring down and surrounding you. Filling you and pouring into the Earth, down to the core of the Earth, if you have it in your mind that it is there; then so it will be because the intent is there.

Many of you can see this light quite clearly, and this is good because the more that you can visualise something, the more powerful it is. As you know, thought can produce many things. Thought is all-powerful, so it is important to use your thoughts for the good of mankind. Keep your thoughts pure always, and then you will be harmless to all. It is harmlessness that is important, and to be of good endeavour, and use your actions and words for the good of all. This ideal has been spread for many years throughout the world, and Sai Baba has used it in India, and he has brought many good things to bear over the years of his life. As you are aware he is a great healer, and He has used his abilities to improve the life of many thousands of young people through his schools and colleges, and his ideals have also been spread to other countries through his endeavours. This idea of harmlessness and being of good endeavour has been utilised to the full by those who have come across his works.

Many are attempting to change their ways at this time. I know that through the years since most of you began to develop your spiritual aspect, by meditating and sending forth healing and light, your lives have changed. You may have found that people that you have known and been extremely close for most of your life, many of these have faded away, and although you keep in contact with them, they are of less importance to you than others who are working with the light, with whom you have only recently been in contact. They are of more importance to you than those you may have been extremely friendly from your youth, and it seems strange that this should happen. Do not concern yourselves unduly, because those with whom you have been friendly over many years obviously do not think and act in the ways that you are working. They may be good people, and I am sure they are, but they have not been extending themselves spiritually, and using this awareness to full effect. They may be of good faith and go to church or whatever temple of worship they use on a regular basis, but they have not reached full spiritual awareness.

It is strange, but this is happening to all of you who are light workers. As I say, do not concern yourselves unduly. Try to plant a seed within their minds that meditation is good for the soul, and that certain ways of worship are perhaps outdated. That it is important to be silent at times, to bring that silence within you so that you can hear that still small voice that is always there, speaking to you within your soul, and tell them that this is all important in this lifetime. If they respond, that will be a wonderful thing, if they do not; you have not hurt them or wasted their time. It will just have given them food for thought, and they may come back to you in time and ask more about meditation and how it can be brought into their lives. It is all up to the individual, but this is a time of great importance to all men who are incarnating at present.

Each one of you is aware that this self-discipline of raising the consciousness is most important, and it is completely necessary for the next stage of your lives. You have been told by many beings, the Masters of the Hierarchy, the Devic Kingdom (this includes the Angelic Hierarchy), beings from space as you call it, from other planets who have been in contact and communication with some of you. Some have channelled books through various individuals, bringing word to humanity about the work that has been continuing over the years. They have been working with the Masters of the Hierarchy and the Angelic stream of consciousness. All of us together have been attempting to bring through these new thoughts to mankind over the years, and at last we feel the time for the breakthrough has come, so mankind can rise upwards and be his true spiritual being at last. He has the capability of expanding his consciousness to be a part of that Universal Consciousness, of which we too are a part, so that we can all be one. We can help you to realise your potential so you, as beings of light can evolve fully into the next dimension of being that is your destiny.

Gradually and imperceptibly you have been evolving over the years, and within a short space of time, all of you will have achieved what you are meant to do, rising upwards into the fourth dimension with the Earth herself, and gradually through that into the fifth dimension. Once you have reached the fourth dimension, you will find that there will be no effort required to move into the fifth dimension within a very short space of time. As Sananda has told you, the fourth dimension is one in which you will be able to see many beings of light, with whom you may have been in contact over the years, but never seen. Some of you may have seen these beings from time to time fleetingly, those who are clairvoyant, but not completely for very long, just glimpses seen and appreciated, but all of you who have been linking with the higher consciousness, and hearing from beings in the ethereal realm will be delighted that you will be able to actually see beings at last after many communications over the past years, including the one who is channelling these words. She has heard from many beings of light over this time, and channelled our communications faithfully for our benefit, and for your benefit, and I know that she will be thrilled to see all of these in time to come.

When first someone begins to channel it is foreign to them, and they perhaps wonder what is happening to them and why they are able to be telepathically in communication with other beings from another realm of life. All of you will have this capacity, if you will, but have the faith and confidence to know that you are capable of this, and will be more so in due course. Before very long, as I have said, you will have the ability to see and hear us. I know that this seems unbelievable perhaps, to you at this time in your lives, but believe me, that capability is not far away, and you have great things to look forward to, and as Sananda said in his last communication, momentous happenings are about to begin. I, Master R, have great pleasure in passing on this wisdom to you, it is something that many of you have doubts about perhaps. It is only human to be filled with doubts, but try to realise what is occurring throughout the world.

I know that there is still violence, cruelty and many sad disasters, fighting and negativity in various parts of the Earth, but I know that you have been trying to pour light into these areas from the Christ Star, and from myself, St Germaine's violet fire of light into these areas, and gradually the light will prevail. You can use this light for your own benefit, and raise yourselves onto that higher dimension of being. It will not take too much effort because already most of you can hear from your guides or other beings, and that still small voice of God who is there for all of you to hear. Just have faith and know that all this will come to pass in a short space of time, and it will all be given to you with God's grace. We are all working together in a great common unity of love and light for all. Peace be with you all this day. God bless.
Master R.

TEACHINGS FROM THE ASCENDED MASTERS-10

I, Master R wish you well, all who read these words. There is so much happening around you at this present time that it is difficult to describe exactly what you are going through, apart from the fact that all of you are attempting to reach within yourselves to hear that still small voice, and to raise your consciousness to an even higher level. This is good and is really necessary at this time in your incarnation. A great time of change and anticipation is abroad. There is a thrill in the atmosphere, because so many of you are aware that it is time for a change to a higher level of being. As I have said, it is a daunting procedure, and I know that many of you have reached that doorway of light in the heavens, and suddenly you wondered what is beyond that door. It is something that you have never experienced before, and which few men have, I say men, women as well, because you have come to the time when your level of consciousness is keeping up with the Earth's progress upwards onto the fourth dimension, and therefore as this has never happened to the Earth previously, it is the same with mankind.

However, you know that you must go with the flow, and be aware of everything that is happening to you and to others. Try to help others who are not on the spiritual path. I am sure that you will be tired of this repetition, but it is only through repetition that you will realise how important these repeated phrases are, help others at this time to realise their true potential through learning meditation. You, and all who read these words have been aware, and have meditated for many years, but this meditation needs to be done twice daily now, at least, so that you will become more spiritual as each day goes by. You have always been spiritual, but this part of your makeup is becoming more important, or as important as the physical, shall we say, and so it must be with all who have the potential to reach the fourth dimension within a short space of time.

This is a time to be bold; it is a time to take that courageous step forward. That large step that needs to be taken, and once done, you will wonder why you were concerned about it, because all of us from the realms of light are encouraging and attempting to guide, comfort and support you as you pass through this threshold. We are there and surrounding you at this time. We will be on the other side of that door in the light waiting for you to join us and become part of the whole once more, when you will be able to do many things that at present you are restricted from doing and creating. Once through that doorway of light, you will recognise how so much has been missing in your lives, and what is invisible to you at present will be shining forth, and all those beings of light with whom you have been in communication over the years, will be before your eyes.

You have been told that in the future, once you have reached that higher dimension, you will see many beautiful beings, the devic kingdom, the angelic hierarchy from time to time, and certainly your guides. All will be revealed to you within a very short space of time, and we, the Masters, will occasionally show ourselves to you as the need arises. I know that we have appeared to some of you in the past, and of course we channel our thoughts through those who are available for this work, and to whom we are most grateful. You are aware that we have encompassed everything that is necessary in many lifetimes. We have come full circle, and we have been helping humanity over the centuries past to overcome his hindrances and misgivings, to be at one with us and to become the being that he is, truly. A being of light and power that is latent within you all, and which will be revealed once you have reached that higher dimension, and from the fourth to the fifth in rapid succession. From the fifth dimension, you will truly be co-creators with God and join us in everything that we are capable of doing and creating.

All of you have in past incarnations been in positions of power from time to time. You have been able to do much good, and have caused what might be called miracles to occur at times during those incarnations, because all of you who read these words have been accomplished, either in temple work, maybe as priests and priestesses in those former lives, working together for the good of mankind wherever you have been, in service to God and humanity. You have been capable of so much more than you are at present, but wait for this giant step forward and then you will have progressed further than you have in any other lifetime. That step is waiting for you to overcome, and so all of you take heed that we from the higher realms are supporting you at this time.

Once you have centred yourselves in your meditations, allow yourselves to rise upwards swiftly, up that beam of light towards the Christ Star, and allow yourselves to become one with us, once you have passed through that doorway of light that is waiting for you. It is a golden doorway beaming out golden light towards you, beckoning you to enter into this new realm of being. Allow this to occur, and just float in through that doorway, accompanied by your guide and whoever you wish to enter the doorway with, and we will be there to welcome you with open arms. All that you have ever wished for will be here, and you and others like you will be present. There is nothing to fear but fear itself, and the violet fire of light that Saint Germain has been pouring down from the heavens has been accomplishing much. You have filled yourselves with this light and it burns away negativity, filling you with confidence and grace, therefore you should be beings of power, who are ready to accomplish anything at this time. Allow yourselves to go with the flow and to be one with us, and become part of the Cosmic Consciousness once you have achieved that goal.

You know that you will return immediately to continue with your lifestyle. I think that some of you wonder what will happen once you have passed through that golden door, will you be able to return? Do no doubt this my friends, all is very well, it is only in meditation that you will be on the fourth dimension. Your body and everything surrounding you the rest of your life will still be here on the third dimension, waiting for your return. As you know, time does not exist here in the realms of light, but your time will continue on the third dimension. It will be frozen into immobility while you are on the fourth and fifth dimensions, so, like the Avatars that exist at this time, Sai Baba and Mother Meera, and perhaps a few more, they can travel onto the fourth and fifth dimensions at will, and yet their bodies continue to function on the third dimension. Therefore, you can exist in two dimensions at one and the same time. I believe that this has been mentioned previously, some time back, but do not concern yourselves that you will be devoid of this life that you are presently living. The two can work together in unison, so that you can exist in this dimension here on Earth, and continue as you have been doing, but the knowledge that you can raise up into a higher dimension and do work there is exciting to say the least! You will find great scope in your new abilities, and be able to help in many ways inconceivable at present. You will be able to create through the mind, and learn to be limitless in your capabilities once you have achieved this step over the threshold into the light beyond.

What is necessary at this time is great faith in our words. We would not speak to you on these things if it were not imminent that you be ready to cross over and be one with us, helping us to achieve more as time progresses. As more of you are able to pass into this new dimension, and yet be part of the third at the same time, there is so much potential for you all, and for us, and we will help you through this process. As you know, many beings are helping humanity at this time, and all of us working together will achieve what you yourselves might not be able to achieve without us and without God's help.

We know that you should always say a prayer before attempting to meditate, and raise your consciousness. It need not be the Lord's Prayer; it can be an invocation, one that has been given to you over the years. So long as you protect yourselves with the light, all will be well. This time of change needs faith and courage, but we know that through your faith and God's help, so much can be achieved, and we will protect you, all of us together working in unity, the Masters of the Hierarchy, Angelic Hierarchy, beings from planets who have great concern with the Earth, and have done over the millennia. They have travelled through time and space as you know, and they are genuine and sincere in their attitude towards mankind.

Once you have achieved this new capability, all of you will be able to see what man has been doing to the planet, and realise how the devic kingdom is concerned. They have been protecting the plants, trees and flowers, and the whole of the Earth over the centuries, and have found that of recent years, their work has been increased so much to overcome the harm that man has done, causing great distress to both the mineral, plant and animal kingdoms through the pollution of the Earth, because the pollution does not only go into the streams, rivers and oceans, it permeates through the rocks, soil and whole of the infrastructure of the planet, thus affecting everything that lives upon it.

You will be able to see this with new eyes once you have achieved this new dimension of being, and you will realise how important it is to pass on this knowledge that mankind must do something very quickly before the Earth herself comes to grief. The Earth will protect herself, but mankind himself may be affected by this protection, and you must understand that although the Earth, Mother Earth, is mother of all, she needs to protect herself. The rivers and streams are her lifeblood, and if they are polluted, they pollute her. I know that all of you are aware of this, but I know that more could be done to maintain a healthy Earth than being done at present. All should know of this, and protect the areas in which they live, passing on this knowledge to all.

Allow yourselves to realise your potential in time to come, and become a true being of the cosmos with us, part of the Universal Mind, and recognise that all of you beings of light have that divinity within which is beginning to shine forth more strongly as the years go by. Shine that light from within you to all with whom you come in contact. Give love wherever it is needed and be ambassadors of love and light to all. God bless.
Master R.

TEACHINGS FROM THE ASCENDED MASTERS-11

This is Master R and I am happy to greet you all this day with a further communication for you. There is so much to think about at this time, this time of great happenings throughout the whole of the Earth. Many people are aware of their true nature, what they are capable of now, and what they will be capable of once they have reached that higher dimension of being. You are true spiritual beings, and your capabilities, once you have gained that new dimension, will be limitless, however there is much to do before then in a short space of time. You have all been working on your meditations, and I hope that they have proved to be fruitful for you, it is a time when mankind will come into his own, and realise his true potential. I know that many of you have thoughts on the subject, doubts perhaps, of your capabilities, but believe me, once you have meditated fully each day, at least twice, your spiritual nature will come to the fore, and you will find that given time, you will be able to be in communication with many beings of light. If you have not already reached this stage, do not worry, because there is so much happening at this time, that even time itself is speeding up.

Many of you may have already noticed this, that over the past years time has speeded by and here you are almost at the end of the year without realising it. I have noticed that most of you who read these words have been aware of this, and have wondered at the speed of time. You know that once you have achieved a higher dimension, there will be no time, as you know it, because time is man made, as you are aware, and that we in the realms of light do not exist in time. We are out of time, and those who have been accessing the fifth dimension, the Avatars, Sai Baba and Mother Meera can use this capability with ease whenever necessary. They can exist on the third and fifth dimensions simultaneously, speeding across the world to be helpful to someone in dire need of their assistance, and yet be working in the third dimension as usual.

It is something that you will soon understand, how time stands still on this third dimension, while you, your spiritual self, are existing on the fifth when necessary, in time to come, but first you must access the fourth dimension that is rapidly approaching. The Earth itself has been rising upwards steadily due mostly to the light workers sending forth light from us and from the Christ Star. You have been helping to fill the Earth with this light from both the Christ Star and myself as Saint Germain, sending the violet fire of light through yourselves and into the core of the Earth. This too has been of great help to the Earth because this violet fire in its burning away of any negativity, doubts or fear through yourselves and the Earth, she herself has benefited from this energy that she has been using to gradually rise upwards. In time, the Earth will be as she should be, a part of the fifth dimension with those other planets who have existed on this dimension over the millennia.

The time has come for this change, as you know, and it is gradually being wrought upon the Earth, and hopefully it will occur without too much upset to yourselves and the rest of humanity. There will be changes of course, as time progresses, but these changes will not affect you unduly, the structure of the Earth will be altering somewhat, but it will not concern you or your loved ones. The main thing to occur that you have to be ready for, is that of the time change, the non-existence of time, that will seem strange to you to begin with, because when you do access a higher dimension, you will feel that much time has passed while you have dwelt there, and spoken to others on that dimension. However, when you return to your physical self, you will discover that it has only been seconds instead of the hours or almost days it might seem to you. Therefore, this adjustment to your way of understanding time can take a little while; it will be a pleasant surprise to you to find that you can achieve much on that higher dimension in a short space of time.

There is much to be done, and you will be able to help us in many ways once you have taken that giant step upwards, and although that step may seem a giant one at present, you must realise that it will happen in a twinkling of an eye once you are ready, and we will be greeting you with open arms because the more who are able to achieve this, the more we can help both you and others. At this time of change, you will be able to assist many people on the threshold to pass over it, and help them understand how this is achieved once you have gone through that doorway to the fourth dimension. You will be able to see what you cannot at present, to be able to understand others in a better way. If you wished to, you could see into their very souls, you will be able to see auras, and the colours involved. Perhaps you will not wish to know others' thoughts, because this is possible. You will be able to read their minds as we can, but it is not essential, and if you do not wish to have this knowledge of your friends, you can ignore it.

Some people are able to do this now. Those who are clairvoyant can see auras as you know, and sometimes they do not wish to see into the hearts of their friends or acquaintances, and therefore they do not use that knowledge to the full, if it is not necessary at the time. Therefore, you too can either access this capability or not, depending on how you feel about it. It may be that you would wish to help someone to achieve higher knowledge, and in this way you can speak to them through your mind, speaking from your higher self to their higher self to pass on this knowledge to them, so that through their subconscious or super conscious mind they can learn, probably during sleep, how it is that they can achieve this higher dimension of being. It is possible to achieve so much more in a short space of time if you use this capability to the full, so that those who are on the brink of awareness can achieve it very quickly in the time allotted to you, because everything as you know, and as I have said, is speeding up, and the time is growing short for mankind to achieve his full spirituality, his full awareness.

Obviously there will be many thousands of people who will not take part in this change of consciousness and dimension. Those men of violence that have been mentioned, all who are working for the darker side will not take part in this. They will be swept aside when you and others pass on to that higher dimension of being with the Earth. They will return to spirit and duly reincarnate on another third dimensional planet when they return to physical life on the wheel of karma, but you who read these words will not need to reincarnate again. You will have achieved what others have not achieved in the past. This is your last incarnation, for your karmic cycle will have been completed in this lifetime, but this lifetime will continue on a higher dimension, and although it may seem strange to you at present, your loved ones will also go with you onto this higher dimension of being, and will not have to continue repaying karma any more.

Life will change so that there is peace throughout the world. There will be no violence once you have achieved this new dimension. It will truly be the new Heaven and Earth that was foretold in the Bible all those centuries ago. The New Jerusalem will have been built in people's minds and on the Earth, once this step into the new dimension has been achieved. I think all of you have realised that these are the latter days, also prophesied in the Bible, and although you may not have read about them recently, it might be worth referring to Revelations in the Bible, what is known as these Revelations are coming to pass. It may not be fully accurate, but when you consider how long ago those words were written, there are certain similarities to what is occurring at present. Also forecast in the past that there will be wars and rumours of wars continually throughout man's existence, but once this fifth dimension is achieved, those wars will have ended, and there will be true peace on Earth, and there will be goodwill towards all men. This is something that I know you have all prayed for, for so many years. Mankind has truly achieved so much in a long space of time, but that time is now coming to an end and wars will finish once and for all.

Satan has been having the time of his life, but his time will be over, and will be banished forever, both from the Earth and from men's hearts and minds. The evil that has been spreading will be ended and negativity will be a thing of the past. There has always been darkness and light upon the Earth, and this has been necessary to enable men to see the error of their ways, and for them to repent of their sins and evil, so that they can repay their karmic errors, and this is what has been occurring over the many incarnations that you have taken part in, but the time has now come for the darkness to end and for the true Golden Age to begin. All of you have so much to look forward to in your lives, and this life is truly one of great achievement for mankind. We wish you well. I will speak again soon. God bless, Master R.

TEACHINGS OF THE ASCENDED MASTERS-12

It is I, Master R, and I greet you this day with rejoicing. I feel that now is the time that many souls are awakening to the fact that they are capable of reaching up to a higher level of consciousness. So many more of you are becoming aware of your true spirituality and true potential as beings of light. It was said that 'Our birth is but a sleep and a forgetting', and these words were true at the time, but this is now the time of awakening. The poet Wordsworth knew what each incarnation meant, and that truly when you return to spirit, that is the time of the awakening of the spirit when it returns to its home, but this present incarnation is truly a time of awakening because you will not need to return, you will not need to make that transition to light again. The normal transition that you call death is a thing of the past for those who have awakened to their true potential, because you will become a part of the macrocosm, the whole Universal Consciousness.

Once you have passed over that threshold of light into the fourth dimension you will truly know what you are. Your spirit will be free, particularly once you have progressed swiftly into the fifth dimension, but even at the beginning when you have crossed that threshold of the fourth dimension, you will see so many things that have been hidden from your view. You will be able to know the real truth, what is in your heart at present and in the hearts of others. You will find that you can read into the hearts and souls of all who you come in contact. Perhaps this will be daunting to you and you may not wish to know the real truth that lies behind those who you know. Your true friends will be revealed to you, and those who may be false friends will be revealed to you also. This is what you feel you may not wish to know, but nevertheless it is there, the truth is there waiting to be revealed whether you like it or not. Sometimes the truth may be something different from what you might expect, and I hope that all your friends are true to you, let no man be false but all be true to their God within.

You and all who read these words know the truth. You are aware, I feel sure that each one of you is loyal and true and would not be false to each other or to God. No one can be false to God because He can read into your hearts and souls, and He knows the truth and has always done. Just remember that what is within you is most important. You are aware of that inner knowing, you are aware of that secret wisdom that lies within the very core of your soul, and most of you are extracting that wisdom now. You are constantly conscious that if you turn within, you may learn real wisdom. As has been said before, there is wisdom written in many books, but if you will turn within, that wisdom is there, and only needs to be turned on like a tap for you to discover the treasure that all of you can have. You only need to have faith that it is there, the treasure of the Ancient Wisdom that lies within your very soul. Sometimes it is difficult to have the confidence to discover this treasure. It is hidden from you for most of your life until the reality dawns, until that spirituality that has been latent there, is fully discovered and explored.

Much of it has lain dormant, and therefore needs awakening like yourselves, and all the others who are still asleep to this fact, but try to bestir all those who need awakening. It is important that they are told at this time, because it is necessary to have all of you fully awakened to all the facts that you yourselves know now, but those facts are latent within those who are still asleep. Your friends and dear ones who through no fault of their own, are perhaps too busy in this lifetime to have the luxury of discovering their true potential. They are too busy with their physical and material lives. Perhaps they have young children, or they have jobs that take up all their time. This is a time when they must learn that they should make time to have a little period of stillness and calm in their lives each day.

Try to awaken in them that truth and this necessity that all require in their lives, even ten minutes of stillness when they can just be themselves. Just BE instead of doing, thinking and listening to sounds that are without, instead of that small voice within, which they are unable to hear because of their busy lives and noise around them. Help them to discover that part of them that is unknown to them and which they are completely ignorant about. Within them is that capability that has been lying dormant the whole of their lives, but it is important, in fact, imperative that all should know this. That seed of knowledge needs to be brought forth planted and blossomed at this time, this time of change and transition for all of you and the Earth, as you know.

What has been arcane knowledge up to now must be passed on to all, so it is your task here to carry out part of God's plan, to pass on this knowledge to everyone. If they disregard it at this time, that is fair enough, but you will have played your part in the plan. You have been passive up till now, but now is the time to stand on your own feet, dare to be different from those whom you have kept this secret. You know in your hearts that many of these people you have come across who are unaware of this wisdom will disregard what you say, but this matters not, the time has come when this knowledge should be known by all. You have been aware for some years that when the time of change comes will be the time you come into your own, and help others through that time to understand what is occurring. That time is fast approaching, and you and others of like mind have the ability to pass on this knowledge that you have been aware of for so long.

You have had a secret life since you have been aware of your spiritual nature. You have kept this knowledge from those who you felt would scoff at your suggestion that they have a spiritual side to them, a side hidden from the physical one. What you have been learning over the past years is something that all men knew at one time, and they accepted as part of their lives. This was when men first incarnated on

Earth, before they gradually became violent and unresponsive to their spiritual nature. Now is the time for men to turn aside from violence and suffering. Now is the time for truth to come to the fore and for all of you to spread the word. I am aware it is difficult to approach this subject with people who do not believe in anything that suggest psychic or telepathic abilities, UFO's, reincarnation, complementary medicine, or any subject that appears to be taboo to them, but which is part of your lives. You have known about esoteric subjects, but realise that other people too have minds of their own, and you would not attempt to impinge your ideas on their minds though you feel strongly that all these topics are true.

However, I am asking all of you to put your faith in what I am saying. It is difficult for you to approach these friends, but I know you will do what you can, to just plant a seed in their minds that things are changing now. We know time on Earth has been speeding up, and they may have noticed and put it down to getting older, or another reason that would suit their ideas, but this can be a start on the subject. I am sure you will find a way to tell them of the changes, and am sure you will find it easy once you begin to explain to your friends and loved ones, and will be capable of much more in time. God bless and keep you.
Master R.

As was given in book one, we shall conclude with this simple Invocation to the Light, which is powerful, that asks for Michael the archangel to be present.

> "Wielder of the Sword of Light come forth.
> Defend man from his darkness.
> May God's pure Divine Light shine through the hearts of men,
> And love and peace prevail."

TEACHINGS FROM THE ASCENDED MASTERS

PART FIVE

TEACHINGS FROM THE MASTERS
Book Five

CONTENTS	Page
Section 1 – Master Jesus/Sananda	164
Section 2 – Master Jesus/Sananda	167
Section 3 – Master Jesus/Sananda	170
Section 4 – Master Jesus/Sananda	173
Section 5 – Master Jesus/Sananda	176
Section 6 – Master Rakoczi	180
Section 7 – Master Rakoczi	183
Section 8 – Master Rakoczi	186
Section 9 – Master Rakoczi	189
Section 10 – Master Rakoczi	193
Section 11 – Master Rakoczi	197
Master R's Invocation	200
FOR THOSE NEW TO CHANNELLING	201
LIST OF FUTURE PUBLICATIONS	202

Channelled by Beryl Charnley

TEACHINGS FROM THE ASCENDED MASTERS-1

My greetings to you and to all who read these words. We start a clean sheet, a new beginning for the New Year, and I hope that the words that I give you will give all of you inspiration for the coming year. There is much to think about when you make a new beginning. What I have in mind is to give you my thoughts on how this year should go. It is hoped that there will be many changes in the thoughts of men for the better.

All of you who work with the light are having an effect on those who have not yet seen the light, shall we say. The light is becoming progressively stronger as you channel it towards you and from you to others, and to those parts of the world who particularly need light at this time, as well as healing and love poured towards them. We from the spiritual realms have, as you know, been working extremely hard to make those changes come to pass, so that your Earth becomes restored again, and peace will come to all throughout the Earth in the near future. As you are aware, there are times when violence seems to spread wherever you look, but this violence will come to an end, believe me. Often it has to become worse before it gets better, so that the whole Earth is cleansed of impurity and negativity. Goodness will prevail, I promise you that.

You have all been feeling that the time has come for the thinning of the veil between the third dimension and the fourth. There have been many changes in outlook, people are becoming more spiritually aware, and at this time of change they are beginning to accept the word which has been given to you, and accept the fact that in time they will be ready to raise upwards on to a high level of being. More people are extremely interested in their spiritual welfare and ready to be taught what is necessary, often it is only a change of attitude, and they will become conscious of this. It is quite easy to change and particularly so if these people wish to improve their capabilities. They only have to bring meditation into their lives on a regular basis, and once that has been established, they will find that they can change themselves without any problem, once they have accomplished the art of meditation as you have.

Meditation is part of your life now; an important part, and I know that you feel deprived if you miss your daily meditation. It is a necessary part of spiritual growth, and once that is part of your life you will never change that routine. It is a discipline that is essential, and a part of the cleansing process that you and others of like mind have achieved over the last few years. A cleansing of the soul and an opening up and expansion of the consciousness, so that you and others like you are raised on to that higher level of being at the time of the meditation. It does not necessarily follow that you remain on that higher level of consciousness. It just means that you have opened the door to spiritual reality, to an expansion of consciousness that all of you find is essential to your being.

Once you have linked with your higher self or the God within, it is impossible to close that door, and it is something that you have searched for all your lives, perhaps unknowingly when you were younger, but some of you who read these words are quite young, and obviously have that inner knowledge which has come from a previous incarnation, to make it simple for you to naturally assume this capability that many take years to learn, it is that of linking with the higher realms through your higher self or your guide. It is important that this capability is improved upon as time progresses, and many people are able to meditate during their daily routine, and can do so when doing their daily chores, for instance.

It is just a matter of switching off the mundane level of thinking and moving into a higher gear, shall we say, so that if you cannot spare time for sitting down in a quiet room for half an hour or more, many of you have reached this capability as a matter of necessity perhaps, and so can switch into this higher level of thinking and being as you work. It is something that those who live in monasteries have achieved over the years, and can meditate constantly as they work. Of course it is easier for them if they are working silently and do not have people conversing with them. However, you can achieve this capability, and if you wish, if you work on your own you can raise into a higher level of being, but naturally not doing this while you are driving the car or doing anything else that may cause danger to others! Naturally it is something that can be worked on as time progresses.

The time ahead will see many more changes come about throughout the world. There will be the changes in climate as usual, and previous times the seasons began to show how difficult it was becoming to know what time of the year it was, and birds and plants were confused, many plants producing flowers at unusual times. As well as the physical changes, spiritual changes will continue to happen. All of you have within you the power to change things yourselves. Of course you can change your lives if you wish to, just through altering your attitude, and you can help to bring about change in others just by gently passing on a little knowledge here and there, that you yourselves have found useful, and hopefully those with whom you come into contact will find that they too wish to change. It is a gradual process, and can be a war of attrition against evil and violence that you may not come across yourselves, but if that light within you is sent forth with great power and intent to all places where the light is required, then you will have brought about a change in that part of the world. Do not feel that as you are a long way from somewhere such as the Middle East or parts of Africa, Northern Ireland and other parts of the world that need help that you cannot do anything. It is not essential to be there to help to change it, all you need to do is send out light and love from your heart towards these areas.

The heart centres of all of you are opening, and becoming much more powerful as time progresses. You may not be aware of this, but I, Sananda, can see this happening and am delighted that all of you have this change within you and the capability of becoming even more powerful beings of light. You have been bringing down the white light and violet fire of light, and the combination of the two is very powerful and will pour down into you and your homes, and loved ones will benefit as will the Earth, but use this light for the good of all. I know that you send it for healing and for the benefit of all these places where there has been violence. Peace is beginning to descend on these places and through our light work we can help to make it extremely safe, so that peace will remain and violence will ebb away and the light will prevail.

St. Germaine's violet fire of light is working well. It is burning away negativity within the Earth and all those places where violence and negativity have been abounding. It is also burning away negativity within you and filling every part of you with grace and inspiration. It is an uplifting light, and will gradually have the effect of working on the Earth, and those of you who work with it in rising on to the fourth dimension, and that light is taking effect on all of you. You may be aware of this, and hopefully you will become part of the fourth dimension very soon. Do not concern yourselves that you may be departing from the Earth and your loved ones because you will not. The Earth herself is rising upwards, and it is a slow process, but gradually she is becoming a part of that fourth dimension. You will find that changes will come about between during these years ahead, and you will look back and realise that you have altered since the previous year. These things are so gradual that they are imperceptible, but nevertheless, all these changes are occurring within you and around you.

Many beings of light are helping at this time, including Michael, who has been spreading light as always, but has become increasingly more powerful over time, in serving both God and mankind in the way that was intended. The light has become much more powerful too as a result of his work, and he is constantly working with me and the Masters of the Hierarchy, and all of us are pleased with the results achieved over time. Invocations have been intoned by many of you and they too have become much more powerful as well. The Great Invocation that was given to mankind has been spread abroad, as a result. Both overseas and in Britain it has become much more generally used, and has great effect on both mankind and his surroundings, and in time to come we feel that it will perhaps be used in churches. I just wish to say that all is well, very well, and as time progresses I hope that these communications will help you and all with whom you come into contact. God bless and keep you this day, Sananda.

TEACHINGS FROM THE ASCENDED MASTERS-2

I, Sananda greet you this day and I wish to speak of various things. Firstly, let me explain how there is an ocean of consciousness in which the planets and stars reside. The whole universe is within that universal consciousness, but it is rather difficult to convey how we speak to one another. It just is so; there is a link between our minds through this ocean of consciousness, a telepathy in which we dwell. It is something that is latent within all men, this capability of linking your minds to the universal mind and to an individual consciousness like my own, to which you can link if you so desire. It is possible to reach upwards to other levels and realms of consciousness, if you are able to go beyond man's normal level, but this is something that must be learnt and it cannot come about without practice. Usually it is those who are on a higher dimension than those on Earth who can reach higher than the consciousness of the Masters.

I have been in communication for some time with this channel, and as a result it is possible for us to link together quite quickly. It is not always possible to convey my full thoughts to anyone on Earth, but I am able to link through her whenever it is necessary. At times we link together outside in the garden, and this is pleasant walking and talking, looking at nature and listening to the birdsong. It is more natural and on a lighter vein of communication, whereas at present I am attempting to give you inspiration that will help you along life's journey. You have progressed so far, and through the years we hope that there will be more communications. Obviously once you have all reached a higher dimension this capability will improve tremendously, but at present I hope to help you as far as I can.

When you are sitting in meditation attempting to listen to another thought process, from your guide, higher self, or that inner voice of God, it is good to attempt to raise your consciousness higher each time. Do this by reaching up through the shaft of light, imagining yourself on a higher level entirely than that of the Earth, so that you meet this other consciousness half way, so to speak. As a result you will become a part of that ocean of universal consciousness, so that it will be easier for you to link together. As time progresses, you will find that you will rise upwards from the mundane level and eventually your consciousness will be permanently raised. You will become a fully integrated part of that consciousness, and as a result you could, if necessary, link with many beings of light who may wish to speak to you in the future. Your guide is always there to protect you and as you are aware, having said a prayer or invocation, you are always fully protected.

That ocean of consciousness has been there from time immemorial, and it links everyone together, so that you become part of the whole and not separated as you normally feel existing in your physical body. Your physical body is of course separate, but your mind can link up with realms above at any time. It has been said before that you can meditate while doing mundane tasks, so that the mind, the spiritual part of you meanwhile, is linking with that universal mind. You can feel as a result that you are truly one with everything because all is one. Nature and mankind should feel that they are part of one another; it is that spiritual light, that web of light that links all beings whatever they are. All the kingdoms of the Earth are one, the nature kingdom that includes all growing things, the animal kingdom, the mineral kingdom and of course humanity who can link with the devic kingdom who link with other kingdoms. They are part of the angelic life stream who reach upwards to their divinity as man does, whose innate divinity that always lives on through each incarnation, and links with all beings who have ever lived.

God created all; He is the one source of all being. It was through God that everything came about, every universe that exists and keeps on expanding forever, was created by Him and He is the link with everything that is and ever shall be. I, Sananda say this, that all beings whether created upon the Earth or whatever planet or star they exist upon, we are all one. Never fear the unknown, never fear the future because the future, present and past all link together as one, and those who live on other dimensions are always aware of this because they can travel through time and space, and have done over the millennia. Therefore that endless belt of time is all a part of universal consciousness, and what is now may have been some time past, or will be in the future, it is all one, so live in the now and think only of the now. Do not concern yourselves with what has happened in the past, that has gone, but the future lies ahead. Do not concern yourselves with the future, always live in the now, and allow yourselves to be swept on into the future without thinking too far ahead.

As time progresses, you will find that if you think in this way you will have no fear, as I have said of the unknown. Those beings who live on other worlds have been helping over the centuries to maintain a presence around the Earth. As you know, some of us have worked together, the Masters and the Angelic Hierarchy all linking together as one, but of different life streams, but this is not important because as I have said, we are all one and we work together in unity for the good of the whole. This is what we hope that you too will consider as part of your destiny for now, and future times, so that you can link with all of us in the future. We have been attempting to raise the consciousness of all beings be they from the Earth or from other planets similar to the Earth. All of us working together so that we can become a universal being, each one of you part of the citizenship of the universe. As such we expect you to be like ourselves, pure of mind and thought, and ready to help all beings of whatever planet or creed, thinking only of being a part of that great universe.

It is a vast thought for you I know, because until you can see all these beings of light and talk with them, it is a step into the unknown for you, and can only link in thought. At present I know that many of you could not conceive of this or even imagine how it could be, but keep it in your minds for the future. As I have said, you are living in the now, so do not dwell on this fact, just think that perhaps it might be feasible for you, and if you feel that this is so, just store it in your subconscious. Acknowledge that you can be a part, a citizen of the universe, and take your rightful place as an integral member of that universal consciousness, playing your part when the time comes to help others who are on a lower level than yourselves, who have not yet reached that point where they can become one with you.

Perhaps this is a new idea for you and difficult to imagine at present, but as I have said, keep it in mind for the future, and we will look forward to the time when all of us can see one another and link with one another in an instant, so that work can be taken on by all of you to join us in helping those who are in need. At present you are using thought for this, and this is good, sending light towards those who have need of help from time to time, the light of healing and of love and peace to all who are suffering in different ways. You have used light for some time as you are all light workers, and that light from the Christ Star has been used over the centuries to help anyone in need. That light which is becoming more powerful on Earth and have been using to good effect. Continue with this work, also using the violet fire of light from St. Germaine, who is sending this forth in abundance to those who use it for the good of all. It too is becoming more powerful, and I know all of you are attempting to use this daily.

What is necessary is for the word to be spread to as many as will receive it. I know that many of you have been opening up new avenues of thought with others who may not have had that knowledge previously, but are ready to receive it, and as time progresses, increasingly more of humanity will become true light workers like yourselves, linking with all who have lit the light throughout the world, and linking with ourselves on the higher realms. Hopefully through the universal mind, that sea of consciousness will become a part of your daily thought, and the light will stream forth towards you even stronger as you become accustomed to the thought that all are one. All beings on all planets and stars throughout this universe, and the others of which you have little knowledge, but that matters not, it is just the expansion of your mind and consciousness that is necessary at this time, to take in this thought and to feel one with all beings.

Try to link each day with that universal mind, and you will find it easier to rise upwards on to that new level of consciousness. I give you my blessing this day and hope that in time to come we will all see one another on that universal consciousness. God bless. Sananda.

TEACHINGS FROM THE ASCENDED MASTERS-3

I, Sananda greet you this day. There is a new generation of young people who are extremely aware spiritually, they are further advanced, many of them than most of you, so that in future times they will be ready to accept the new and discard the old with pleasure. The old that is being overtaken with changes that are occurring now, and have been happening for some time.

You have been aware of those climate changes for some time, and everything that is occurring links to what will happen in time. There will be changes in the minds of men that will overcome the old negativity and will dominate everything that is violent at this time, dominate with the power of good, light and love. All of you to whom these words are addressed have been working with light and love for some time, but the young people who will come after you and are at present joining with you in this work will have much more power to work with. They will be true channels of light, and be more like those who lived on the Earth when first man inhabited the Earth. They will be in close contact with God and will do His work without any problems or doubts.

It will be a completely new Golden Age for mankind, and the doom and gloom that exists at present will be banished forever. It will be a time of peace and mankind will change his ways completely. I have said in the past that when this change comes about, the Earth herself may have problems. It is when you have risen onto the fourth and fifth dimensions that some disasters happen upon the Earth. The occasional cataclysm when those who have to be swept aside will pass into their spirit forms, but all of you who are working with the light will be quite safe and protected at this time. Once it has occurred there will be no more dominance by violent people, and the governments of the Earth will work for true peace throughout the whole world. You may not comprehend how this will come about, but this matters not because it is not for you to worry about. It will happen, believe me, and we have been working to this end for quite some time.

As you know, the Masters and Angelic Hierarchy together have been attempting to create peace within the Earth and other planets. Also those beings from other planets who have been travelling around Earth for some time helping us, will continue to do so, they are also helping other planets together with ourselves. We are all forming a true network of peace upon the Earth, and it will not be long before that peace occurs. It is difficult to weigh up exactly when it will happen because time to us is non-existent. We are out of time as you know, but try to be patient and just accept these words as the truth that they are. Everything that will occur at that time has been ordained, and as you know in the Bible, much was foretold for the future, and is beginning to happen.

Even in those days there were prophets rather like Nostradamus who have been true seers, and have foretold the future, that in biblical language is sometimes difficult to weigh up. The wording is strange to modern ears, but if you read certain prophets, you will discover these truths and will marvel in your minds as to how they spoke about the future in those days, not knowing anything about modern life, in fact, nothing about how you live now, but their words are coming true. Nevertheless, in the future there will be prophets once more, who will foretell what will come in perhaps another thousand years. Who knows what will occur, perhaps we do, but we do not wish to tell you too much before it happens, otherwise you would be like puppets on a string and just do what we wish, whereas you have your own free will and can do whatever you want to. Although I am sure that will entail nothing negative, but attempt to continue as you have been, following the spiritual path.

The future for mankind is good. You have been told many times that you are gradually rising on to a higher dimension of living, and the Earth herself as she rises is beginning to take on a new feeling. You will be aware that the Earth herself as she rises is responding to all the healing. You will be aware that the Earth is blossoming forth in a way that has never happened before. It is a subtle method of blossoming and therefore it will just occur almost imperceptibly, but you will be aware of a change, which will be occurring to yourselves also. With this change there is a gradual alteration in temperature throughout the Earth. Maybe at present, having had a severe winter here you will not credit this, but the Earth will continue to get warmer, and despite some places receiving more rainfall than usual while others have had drought, the overall effect is that the Earth is getting warmer, overall.

I know that you are aware that there are holes in the ozone layer and probably scientists will obviously use this as an excuse to suggest that this is the cause, but in time it will be found that the increase in temperature although gradual, will become worldwide, so that places that are quite cold will become more temperate. You will find yourselves that although it may take several years, those changes are more than the climate, for it involves a heightened awareness, either within you or the very atmosphere itself, almost waiting for something to occur in an exhilarated way. Perhaps you may think this strange, but you will become aware of this alteration and realise what I mean. It is rather difficult to describe, but in time there will be that heightened awareness within each one of you, so that you will gradually be able to see spiritual beings as you rise upwards. This ascension is not physical but spiritual, and I know that you have known of this for some time, but gradually it will occur and it is not necessary for you to work on it too hard.

Perhaps while some of you have been attempting to meditate, you have been disappointed that you have not yet managed to find your way through that golden door, rising upwards on a shaft of light. It all takes time, and I think that maybe you have been trying too hard. Just allow this to happen gradually as you meditate, and let it be a natural occurrence, so that the mind is not used too forcibly, let your consciousness rise on to that higher level naturally without effort. All of you who are working with the light are using the violet fire of light from St Germaine, and that will help you to rise up to a spiritual level, which you had not achieved previously. Your bodies will be filled with this violet fire of light, and any negativity within you will be dissolved, and you will gradually find that through working with this and the Christ Light, your bodies will become subtler and less physical as time progresses. Everything around you is gradually changing and the veil is thinning between the dimensions.

Children that are growing up at this time will fully comprehend what is occurring and just accept it. They still have that knowledge within them from the spiritual realms, and more of them are retaining that knowledge for longer than they used to. It was always said that children trail clouds of glory, and that glory is from the spiritual realms, and normally by the age of five they would have lost this capability because that is the way of the world, but nowadays they are retaining that capability longer than they did. Therefore their minds will be aware of that knowledge that they brought with them, such as an awareness of spiritual beings, often they are small devas or fairy people, and these beings will still be real to them. Over the years to come, they will develop that capability of clear sightedness, clairvoyance or telepathy, which your generation is attempting to develop, but it is much easier to do this from an earlier age. So those young people will grow up being capable of much more than you, although some of you have been learning much over the years, and are beginning to take your place as channels for those of us from the realms of light.

Try to accept the possibility of many more things to occur in the future. Open your minds to many new thoughts and ideas of your capabilities that are truly endless. Allow these capabilities to improve and you will be surprised at what you are able to do. Believe in miracles and they will happen. Have faith and we will be able to help you through this time of change into the new Golden Age of the future. God bless and keep you all. Sananda.

TEACHINGS FROM THE ASCENDED MASTERS-4

My greetings to you this day, this is Sananda. I think in your minds you have compartmentalised all the beings who contact anyone on Earth. I know that it is natural because you assume that I, Sananda who was Jesus, is automatically connected with the Trinity, and that I and the Archangels work hand in hand together with the Masters of the Hierarchy, in order that mankind may benefit from any help that we may give and have done throughout history. Try not to keep us separate from all the other beings of light who exist in the cosmos, their love is also given to you freely and unconditionally, and we work hand in hand with them also. The beings who live on other planets who work for the good of all, and who have within them a great love for every being that exists. Perhaps you may think that as we have been mentioned in the Bible, meaning the Hierarchy of the Trinity, the Archangels working together and the Masters who have been mentioned over more recent years, and so we are kept separate in your minds. But believe me, we have always worked with extraterrestrials as you call them; they are like yourselves, all part of the whole.

The cosmos consists of galaxies beyond even the knowledge of mankind, the universe is so vast, but think of yourselves as a tiny part of that and then you will realise that you too are extraterrestrials, shall we say, to those on other planets. But assuming that all planets and stars that have beings living upon them are working together, you will find that you belong to that great Hierarchy of cosmic beings, and we have been working together since long before I lived as Jesus in biblical times. Previous to my life in that incarnation there have been visitations upon planet Earth, which have been experienced by mankind in the past, and these visitors were assumed to be gods, because although they were not, they were so evolved both technologically and spiritually, that it was assumed they were gods to those simple people. Over the millennia such landings have occurred quite regularly by other beings from throughout the cosmos and although nowadays it does not happen very often, there are craft seen in the skies above and there have been occasional landings of recent years just in order to facilitate knowledge to be gained by these extraterrestrials regarding the Earth and those who live on it, so that there can be help given whenever required.

You have been aware, of course, for some time that the Earth is gradually changing, and that in due course there will be an ascension. You are aware that the fourth dimension is becoming very close, and that the Earth herself will be rising onto that very shortly. It has been a gradual process over these past few years and will continue; also you are finding that there has been an acceleration of change all about you. Change is always necessary for evolvement, both of thought processes and spiritual development, and also this change is much more dramatic than has been known on the Earth at any other time, apart from the natural changes which have occurred over the millennia, geological changes, climactic changes, the ice age for instance, and over the years more recently, the climate has been changing and will continue to do so, but we have spoken of that before.

Today I am talking about spiritual change that which is less obvious, but this is occurring to all of you. All of you are awakening and attempting to awaken others to their spiritual nature, that spirituality that has been latent and which must be awakened fully. You have within you great power, it is just beginning to emerge and it must come forth over the next few years. All of you are aware of this now, and are attempting to raise your consciousness to an even higher level through your meditations. This will suddenly develop and you will discover new horizons that you had not imagined. You have been trying to conceive how it will be once you have achieved the fourth and fifth dimensions, but your minds at present are limited, and it will be a little while before you emerge from that chrysalis that you are still trapped inside. That butterfly that is waiting will take off in a short space of time, and you will realise how different things will be once this happens.

The light that you have been using and working with over the years is beginning to take effect. You have been bringing it from the Christ Star to pour down through you into the Earth, and from St Germaine, that Violet Fire of Light, so that both the white light of the Christ Star and the Violet Fire have been taking effect within you and within the Earth. That light is now causing a sea change within you that will suddenly alter your capabilities. You will be a truly cosmic being which will be capable of achieving miraculous happenings. Your lives will alter and those around you will be affected, but you need not worry that you will suddenly appear to look different and altered in any respect. Not suddenly developing a beak or horns, shall we say! Do not worry, but the alteration will be quite dramatic, and you will have gained much more authority in order to explain what is happening on the Earth at this time to those who are still unawakened. They will accept what you have to tell them, because unless they do, they will be too late to change their ways and evolve their spirituality fast enough for the change that is about to happen.

New humanity will be taking charge of the Earth, taking charge of the lives of those who are precious to God. All men are, but those who are capable of achieving that new spirituality are particularly precious and will be given that authority to help all with whom they come into contact. More and more of you are becoming aware. There are more even than you would imagine, that are living their lives out around you and who you have not spoken to on this subject. Try to sound out all who you know and see if they are awakened, this is becoming more important and inevitable as time goes on. Those who are quite young incarnating into this world at this time are mostly very old souls who are experienced and have lived many lifetimes. They are born with much more knowledge than even you have after years of meditation and reading many books on spiritual subjects. You will find that the young ones will be able to give their knowledge and help when the important times of the Earth changes start occurring. All will be well because so many of you are ready to help at this time.

You know the phrase 'man know thyself and thou shalt know the universe'. Mankind is beginning to discover himself and what is latent within him, and that wisdom will pour forth and help all of you over the years to come, and then you will be able to join in with all of us throughout the cosmos who are pouring forth our energies to help you to open your minds to that reality that is all around you. Just allow this to occur naturally, it will happen, believe me. I know that many of you are waiting for this new beginning and look forward to what you will be able to achieve, particularly in seeing those who are unseen at present, but of whom you are aware, particularly those who channel our words but cannot see us. They only have the faith to know that we are here helping and guiding all of you always, so never feel that you are alone and helpless. You know that we are supporting you in this new consciousness. All you have to do is go with the flow.

Know that you will achieve your new capabilities that are gradually increasing, and if you believe in me, Sananda, the Masters, the Angelic Hierarchy, and above all, God, you will know that all is well and that we are all working towards the goal of your new consciousness that is just around the corner. All of you who read these words will achieve much in these next years, and you will be surprised when you look back on this time and recognise that my words are true. Go with God. God bless all of you. Sananda.

TEACHINGS FROM THE ASCENDED MASTERS-5

I am happy to greet you this day, this is Sananda. There are so many things to talk of but today I wish to speak about man and his destiny, the future of mankind, because as you may have realised, this is the last incarnation of man. The wheel of rebirth is coming to an end and as a result there will be no more karma, self-imposed karma to be repaid. Whatever karma is caused must be repaid immediately. For instance, if someone commits a sin of some kind in this lifetime, then that karma should be repaid immediately by a kind deed. Instead of waiting to repay it in another subsequent lifetime, which is usual, it must be repaid now and man as a result will find that the violence occurring on the Earth has been increasing. The Age of Kali is nearly ended and the Golden Age that has been promised for so long is finally on its way, but not before there is more disruption, because until there is a storm, there cannot be calm, so the storm is still on the horizon, so to speak.

There have been many occurrences that were devastating to you all, for instance, the many hardships and suffering for children as a result for man's greed for power. This has continued since humanity began over many thousands of years ago, and hardships have been suffered by innocents, but this time, when the changes occur and the Earth finally reaches its higher dimension, those on it who are raising upwards to that fourth and fifth dimension will find that gradually this violence is going to end, and man's destiny looks good.

All of you have been meditating as much as you can and raising your consciousness onto a higher level. It is the vibratory rate that needs to be quickened, so that all of you will be vibrating at a faster rate, rather like the birds and insects who speed across the ether. You will find that you too will be eventually moving at a faster rate. Not obviously, as at present you watch the birds flitting to and fro, but it will be a gradual process as you learn to resonate at that higher vibratory level. All of you are gradually increasing this, but it is imperceptible, so you are perhaps unaware of it. It will only be when you do finally reach that higher dimension that you will look back and realise that you have achieved a higher frequency, when you see others who are still on the third dimensional level, as you will be working between the two dimensions you will appreciate that there is a difference.

At present you are feeling perhaps a little frustrated that you have not yet mastered that achievement that you have been attempting, but keep on with your work and you will be rewarded in time. Everything comes when you are ready for it. Just attempt to go with the flow, do not try to rush anything because the time is not right, you must work in God's time, and work with Him, rather than trying to go against the flood tide. You will find that if you do this, nothing goes right, you must work with God, because you are nothing without Him.

All of you know this in your heart of hearts, but it is only natural that you wish to improve your capabilities.

I think that more of you are attempting to speak to others about their spirituality, and attempting to sow a few seeds here and there, seeds of knowledge, and yet sometimes it falls on stony ground, as you know. At least you are attempting to spread the word when you can. It is important that this is done, because time is passing quickly, and although you may not be aware of it, that time is all-important for those who have not yet spiritually awakened. The spiritual renaissance that has been developing over the last two decades has taken off and soon all of you will be united in your new capability of rising on to the higher dimensions.

Your brothers from other planets have been attempting to contact many of you, and have been trying to help whenever possible to raise that vibratory level through the communications. They have been on higher dimensions from hundreds up to thousands of years. It depends on which planet or star they are from, but all are extremely spiritually evolved, and like yourselves, are beings of light, but have been trapped in these third dimension conditions, which you chose to do before you incarnated. Now you are beginning to discover the size of your being, you will appreciate that they can see what you are in reality, and are helping you to emerge as I have said before, like a butterfly from its chrysalis. To fly and be capable of doing what you were able to do before you incarnated, and which you will do soon when the time comes. They themselves have been on these higher dimensions for so long, they can appreciate how you feel trapped when you try to reach your consciousness higher and higher, but have not yet achieved that leap into the unknown, or it seems to you that it is unknown, because you have been on this third dimensional world for so long.

But realise that you have that potential within you of many things, one of which is the knowledge of the universe, the Wisdom of the Ancients that is locked within you. It just needs the key to turn and all will be revealed unto you, and also many other things that will come to you in time. So it is important for that knowledge to be unlocked, and for the knowledge within others to be unlocked too, those who have not yet awakened to their spirituality, and the discovery that they are beings of light and need to be released.

All of you have been reading books on many subjects related to this new awakening of mankind, and from time to time I know that you have wearied of it, some of you, because you feel that you have not achieved very much, but do not feel disillusioned in any way. You are all improving in your capabilities, although at times you feel that you are not getting anywhere. You will realise when you make that leap on to the fourth dimension, and then the fifth, that it has all been happening slowly but surely, and the time will come soon when the changes occur with all of you. From time to time many of you are aware of what someone is going to say before it is said, or you perhaps hear the phone and you know who will be speaking to you from the other end. All these chance intuitive thoughts are coming to you more and more, and this shows that your spirituality is coming to the fore, and you are using that knowledge that is gradually seeping out from within you into your conscious mind.

So the destiny of man is to overcome this third dimensional world and rise with the Earth, helping the Earth through your light working techniques. That is the plan, God's plan for mankind that is foretold in the Great Invocation, and to bring light and love, and you will take your place in that Plan. All is working out and you and all other lightworkers are doing what is set forth to do in this incarnation, although you could not remember this plan because your minds being blinkered until now. This was your destiny to help the Earth and all upon it to rise onto that higher dimension, and vibrate at that higher frequency, and become a part of the cosmic world. You and others like you are playing that part and gradually the light is taking effect, raising that Earth that you love so much, that beautiful planet on which I lived as Jesus.

I, Sananda, the Masters, the Hierarchy of Angels, and those beings of light from space are uniting as one with you, and we hope that before long, the Earth will participate with all of the planets who have been waiting to take part with the Earth to unify all consciousness, so that we can all participate in a cosmic journey. All of us working for the good of the whole as part of God's Plan, and once we have all united on that higher dimension, the Earth can really play her part, and all of you will participate with us in this, joining forces as one. It is most important for this to occur because the Earth is necessary even though the universe is so vast. For if the Earth were to come to an end, if man turned his back on his spirituality, then it would affect so many planets and stars around, that there would be devastation in that area of the universe. So, it is important for man to use his spirituality, and use the light from the Christ Star, and from St Germaine to help the Earth to rise. We are all anticipating that this will happen in a short space of time.

Mankind will be capable of travelling without the bulky vehicles that he presently needs, and air travel will be easy also. The fossil fuels will be redundant and other means will be employed for air and space travel. All these changes will happen very quickly, and inspiration will be given to those working on aircraft and spacecraft. The new techniques will come about, and all will be capable of travelling great distances in a short space of time, so that apart from teleportation, which will be a normal procedure, and a way of visiting people at a distance, you will find that there will be a greater freedom, and you will have changed lives, all of you as time progresses. All this will be accepted joyfully when the time comes. There will be so much more time for leisure, and people will not be pressurised in their employment. The time will be used to be with their families, and all will change over time so that mankind will develop into gentler individuals, and the greed for power will end.

The time of change is nigh, and we look forward to seeing how things will change for the better for everyone throughout the whole of the Earth. We give you our blessing this day, and the hope for new things to come. God bless you all, Sananda.

TEACHINGS FROM THE ASCENDED MASTERS-6

Greetings dear brothers and sisters of the Light, this is Master R, known at times as St Germaine. I work with the violet flame, and I know that most of you are using this fire presently, which is very powerful. Use it to the full, fill yourselves with this fire, and bring it down through you into the Earth below. This most powerful light will lift you and raise your consciousness on to that higher level, which is necessary for now and the future.

The Masters of the Hierarchy and the Angelic Hierarchy have been working, as you know, with beings from space to help mankind and beings on other third dimensional planets, and to enable all of you to work with the light. In the past you have been using the light from the Christ Star, and it is also important to continue using this light for the benefit of the whole. All of us are working in service with God, and as you know, your planet is the planet of choice, the planet of free will. It is on its own in that respect, the beings from the Pleiades and Arcturus to mention only two groups, as you know there are many beings from other planets who are working in the light, and all of them are following God's will, rather than their own. Service, that is their life, to serve others rather than themselves, therefore they are truly benign beings, and wish only to be your brothers and sisters. Some of you are aware of this, aware of them, but most of you just know within your hearts that this is so, and you hope that one day once you have raised on to that higher dimension of being to be able to both see and hear them. Also to be able to see and hear us, Sananda and myself, and all who work with me, know that this will be so for those who wish it.

Of course, time is something else, as you know. It is entirely man-made, and is non existent to us, but we must try to observe your methods of thinking, so that we can work with you in this respect, and try to guide you in every way onto that higher level of being. As you have been aware for some time, you know that it is most important to link with us through meditation, or to link with your guide or higher self in order to raise the consciousness, and it is that which will lead you through and over the next threshold. You know that there are portals that have opened throughout the world, leading to knowledge of higher worlds. It is through these portals, these gateways that you must pass, in order to gain this knowledge, and to gain the new vibration. By this I mean that you will have passed over the threshold into the fourth and fifth dimensions, and it is these portals that give you access to this. There are several that have been opened, and there are certain humans who have succeeded in raising their consciousness sufficiently to pass through these portals of light, and we only wait for the majority of mankind who are lightworkers to join these favoured few, shall we say.

I know that many of you cannot wait for this time, you long for the exhilaration that you anticipate, once you have reached this capability, because it has been promised for so long, and you feel that it will be miraculous when it does occur. Try not to anticipate it too soon, it has to be worked for, and you have to be ready to enter that rarefied atmosphere. Your body, mind and soul must be in a higher gear, shall we say, moved and accelerated into that higher vibration, rather like a car which, when you have reached the top of a hill, is ready to be moved into a higher gear. As you reach the top of that hill in your life, and move the gear lever to raise you onto that higher level, then you and especially that part of you that is the one that continues through the different incarnations, must be ready to enter that rarefied condition. So do not be impatient my dear ones, just wait until everything is right for you. You must be in the right place, and be in the right way of thinking. Just try to be, and not do so much in your lives. It is only through this that you will recognise that what is missing in your life is that ability of linking with ourselves more readily, and more constantly.

So many people think that they must fill their lives doing things all the time, rushing about and meeting with others, not necessarily of like mind, but enjoying every minute to the full, or they may think they are enjoying themselves. It is only once you have achieved that oneness with us, that you will realise that enjoyment can be in many ways. It is good to meet with others and have laughter and fun from time to time. This is part of your physical life, and it is good to raise the atmosphere on to one of levity, but it is not necessary to fill every moment of the day doing instead of being. After all, you are living in a physical body, but your soul, your very being is confined on to the material plane at present. You are spiritual beings entrapped in the physical vehicle at present, however, it is important for that spirit to join with others, and not be constantly thought of as physical. You are vast beings of light, you are far brighter and glowing than you could ever imagine. We can see your light, we are aware of your capabilities, and we can tell by the incandescent glow coming from you as to what level of consciousness you have reached. It is vital that you keep that light alive, and it is only through meditation and linking with higher worlds that this can occur. So shine your light towards us, and towards others at all times. We are always waiting for that link, and we are ready to guide you on your way.

Picture, if you will, a man stranded on a desert island. He knows that he is alone. He knows that there are no other humans or physical beings on that island, and yet if you will imagine him seeing himself as a being of light and sitting, quietly attempting to join forces with other light beings, then he will recognise that he is never alone. Apart from his own guide, higher self and guardian angel, he can link through thought, prayer and meditation with many beings. There may be other beings on that island who are living there, whom he has not the eyes to see. They could be beings from another planet on that higher dimension that they live upon, and they could be there to help and guide him if he will but listen and have the knowledge that he is not alone at any time. So, he need not despair if he will have faith and know that help will be given to him. It is just an analogy, but it just shows that wherever you are in life, and at whatever stage, you should always know that we can help and guide you through difficult times, and at those times when you perhaps doubt that you will never be able to raise your consciousness sufficiently to reach that higher plane of existence. Do not doubt, never despair, always work with the light and we will be here to guide you.

Use the violet fire of light, allow it to pour down through you, swirling through you with great power to burn away any negativity, doubts or fears that linger within your mind. It is very powerful and will help you and others, and if you will bring it through you into the Earth below you, know that you are helping the Earth herself to throw off any negativity, and for her too to rise up on to that higher vibration that is gradually occurring. You know that energies have been released to enable an acceleration of mankind's capabilities in raising the consciousness of many who have been asleep until now, but are gradually awakening, and are clamouring to learn more. There is much happening at this time, and I am sure that you are aware that more people are ready to learn everything that you have been learning over the last few years.

Everything is accelerating and you will find that very soon there will be vast change in the thoughts of men. You yourselves are a part of the Plan, and you are playing your part in working with the light, and encouraging others to join you in this work. It is not always necessary to work in large groups. It depends on the individual, but whatever you do, we know that you are doing it to the best of your ability, and you are a cog in the wheel. All these cogs and wheels are turning, and coming together as a vast piece of machinery, and all is working together and oiled with the light from the Christ Star and the Violet Fire. You are a part of this, and remember that you are important. You have a part to play, and everything that is happening is God's will. The Earth and all upon her are travelling through an important historical time. Remember this, and know that you are living in a time of great change. It is a time of great happenings, and you and all who work with you are a team. This team is working towards the evolvement of the souls of men, and we ourselves hope that you will continue to work with us; we have much more to tell you in the future. God bless and keep you all. Master R.

TEACHINGS FROM THE ASCENDED MASTERS-7

My greetings to you, this is Master R. As I have said before, this is a time of great change, and those who are on the spiritual path at this time are finding that it is not easy. It may be a time of great joy, and it is wonderful to be on the physical plane at this time, but it is difficult to be on the spiritual path and to be convincing to those who are not yet aware of their true spirituality. You feel that you are part of a secret army attempting to bring light down and spread love wherever it is most needed. It is something that you wish you could tell all, and yet you must out of necessity, keep much of it to yourselves, apart from like-minded people, of whom you aware.

Change is all around you; the Earth herself is rapidly changing, and although you may not be completely aware of it, everyone upon it is changing. You who are on the spiritual path and are lightworkers, are finding it easier to go with the flow, and to assimilate those energies that are being poured down into you, and into the Earth at this time, so that you can be given the ability to change without too much effort. There will be changes in your physical structure, and as you have been aware sometimes, there is some pain that goes with this. Nothing that lasts too long fortunately, but it is something that most of you have felt from time to time, the changes in your muscles and bones that will be in time more ephemeral and less solid. You may have experienced some pain like headaches occasionally, so this discomfort will be something that all of you will have to go through in order to alter the structure of your bodies.

Nothing like this has happened in the past, it is something that has been gradually and imperceptibly occurring over the last few years. Sometimes you may feel lost, and wonder how to do simple daily tasks, and you may also find that your mind is less clear, and you feel rather muddled, then everything will be as it was, and you will wonder what happened. Just accept this as part of the change, and do not worry unduly that your mind is failing you. It is something that is occurring to everyone at this time, it will just be fleeting for a few minutes or seconds, but it is all part of the process of change, and you must just accept this as part of the change.

Everyone on the spiritual path will be going through this, and you will be able to compare notes with others. I know that it is something that you may not wish to broach because you may think that it is just you, but you will find that everyone has had this feeling at some time or another. Maybe over a week or just momentarily, but it will reassure you when you find that each one of you has experienced something of this kind. It is not necessarily only those who are getting older. Many young people have experienced this loss of memory, or mixed up feeling, about everyday occurrences. You will find that it will be straightforward after a little while, if you accept this change, and just go with the flow, it will be easier for you. Realise that we are helping you, and the Angelic forces are also here to give you healing, and to help with this process of change in every way. You may be aware of Angelic forces around you, and you will know that they only wish to serve both you and God. This is all part of His plan for mankind, and you will be aware that the changes within you and around you are only minute compared with the overall plan that He has for the whole of the universe. As I said before, you are very small cogs in the great machinery of life, and everything has to go smoothly, well oiled, working together in unity for the good of all. As I said, you are part of that plan, and you are an important factor in carrying out this great change.

There are inter-dimensional beings who are working with the Angelic force, who are also feeling the change themselves. They are working together to help humanity, and to help many other beings on other planets and stars. There is great activity between the planets and the dimensions. All is occurring at this time, and you, although you are not aware of it, must integrate with the whole, so we, the Masters of the Hierarchy, have been linking with mankind to help him understand that this plan that is happening, is rapidly accelerating at present. I know that you have been told many times that you are becoming fourth dimensional beings, and this is true. It all takes time, but time on Earth is accelerating, and eventually you will realise that the changes that are now occurring are nothing to what will happen in the future. It is all change for the better, and your lives will take on a new meaning.

You will be capable of things that mankind has not been able to achieve before, like Jesus and Buddha and other Avatars who have been able to create these miraculous occurrences. In the future as Jesus said, all these things you too will do, and you will be taking part in this, life will change so that you will be true spiritual beings on a physical world. The changes that will occur will mean that your lives will be as if you were Gods, immortal, you will never die. You will not need to incarnate again, as the wheel of karma has come full circle, or it will have done, this I promise. Naturally, some will pass into the world of spirit before the end of the century, those who are elderly, sick, or have been killed outright by accident or mishap. This will continue as it always has done, but as you rise onto that higher dimension of being, your physical bodies as they change, will become less physical and more amorphous, and you will be able to leap into the fifth dimension when there is danger. It is something that at present you find hard to believe, but it is true that this is gradually happening, and you will be truly beings of light.

When you meditate, use your mind in a more powerful way. You have been bringing down the Christ Light and the light from St Germaine, using this light for healing and projecting into the Earth to fill her with this powerful beam. Use your minds to the full, because the thought process is going to be much more powerful in the future. Your thought will be used instead of your speech. You will find that each one of you will become telepaths, and you will find that you can project your thoughts to others in time, but use that thought for good, always using it for the benefit of all, projecting light into the dark areas where there is oppression and suffering. The world has been going through a time of suffering and violence, and as this continues; you will find that the violence will gradually cease through your thought projection of the light. Send love into those areas and you will find that in time, all the violence and oppression will come to a halt.

The forces of light are working to eradicate the darkness, but this takes time, and it means that all men will have to see the light. All men will have to come to God, and it will take something catastrophic to alter the thoughts of certain branches of humanity such as the I.R.A. and those working together in violence in other parts of the world to devastate and annihilate. They do it supposedly in the name of religion, but they truly are evil and will have to alter their ways or eventually pass into spirit before humanity can all come together in peace. You know that where there is light there is always dark, but eventually that darkness will be prevailed upon, and become less and less. This is what God has planned and although mankind has free will, eventually he will choose good rather than evil, so that in time, the Earth will become a planet where peace will prevail, as it does on the other higher dimensional planets. They have civilisations that have withstood evil over the past centuries, and their lives changed irrevocably as a result, and they hope that their presence here will help humanity to change in the way their did centuries ago. There has been peace upon those planets for so long, they have no memory of wars and violence as the Earth does.

So, fill yourselves with the Christ Light, and know that all will be well. That light will light up the hearts of all of you, and bring peace wherever it touches. You have much to look forward to; this time of change is one of great exhilaration. It is a great time to be alive, and to know that all who live upon the Earth at present will experience that wonderful change in their lives, which will make this world a beautiful planet of peace. I give you my blessing this day and wish you well. Master R.

TEACHINGS FROM THE ASCENDED MASTERS-8

My greetings to you, this is Master R. I wish to speak of the many changes that will be occurring within the years ahead. It is always difficult for us to pin down a time for things to occur upon the Earth and the cosmos surrounding it, but as far as we can see from now until the end of next year, there will be vast changes occurring both to humanity and the Earth, that is heading towards the photon belt. Photons are electrons that react one against the other and create energy. Matter and anti-matter, as you know, cannot live in the same vicinity, and once this area reaches the Earth, both are heading towards one another, in time the photon belt will envelop the Earth, but do not worry for all is organised for you. We, the Masters and various beings from the universe, have been working to create a safe area for the Earth and the Solar System to voyage within this photon belt when the time comes, and together we have created this space that will bring you safely through the time that you spend in this great belt of photon energy.

During the first phase that the Earth passes into this belt there will be darkness for several days, but do not concern yourselves because all is prepared for you, and although the stars will disappear for that short space of time of four or five days, and the sun will not be able to penetrate the belt for that length of time, nor the moon by night. After four days you will see these bright stars and your moon and sun will reappear. There will be a certain coldness obviously, because of the lack of sunshine, and your electrical systems will not function, nor will vehicles be usable, but after that length of time, you will find that there is new power to be utilised in photon energy instead of electrical impulses. The photon energy will spark off new abilities in man, and you will find that your bodies will be subtly changed. You have been told that you will be more amorphous and ethereal when you move onto that higher dimension. Well, this photon energy will provide the energy to lift you onto the fourth and subsequently the fifth dimension within a very short time, and you will be able to do things you could not dream of at present.

You will be able to travel through thought, as has been mentioned before, and this will occur very swiftly after passing into this area. You will find that the energy from the photon beam will give you the ability to heat food, and do all manner of things where you normally use electricity, to cook, and heat your food and homes. In future after this passage of time, you will find you no longer need electricity, nor will it work once the photon energy is around you. Everything will be altered, and you will feel light. You will still be in a physical body, but you will feel changed in many ways. Your psychic and telepathic abilities will increase tenfold, and you will find that gradually everything that has been latent in humanity in this respect will surface, and be more important than anything else. Materialism will be a thing of the past, and you will find life will take on a new meaning for all who experience this new way of living.

As I say, I know that many who are unaware of this may feel threatened and frightened when it does occur, so we depend on you and those who are aware of their spirituality, who will be reading these words to take everyone under their wing, and try to explain what is occurring. It may be that children will be frightened particularly, when for a few days it suddenly begins to get dark for the whole time, not just at night, but throughout the whole twenty-four hours. However, as I have said, it is only for a very limited time, and after three or four days there will be light dawning, the sun will break through, and all will be as it was before as regards your twelve hour day and twelve hour night, but apart from that, everything will feel different about the Earth, the plants, animals and yourselves. Many other beings will be visible to you that were not previously seen. Those who walked the Earth and passed on into spirit will be visible to you, and you will recognise loved ones who perhaps you have heard from or seen fleetingly if you are clairaudient or clairvoyant, but now will be able to see them for a short space of time.

When you move into the fifth dimension, you will then be able to see many beings who have spoken through channels, either guides and guardian angels, or Masters of the Hierarchy. Angels and archangels will also be seen when this time comes, and the entire Devic kingdom will appear to your bewildered and delighted eyes. I think that you will find that much will be revealed that at present you still do not imagine could happen. It is not just the sight of all these beings plus those who walk amongst you who are from other planets, your brothers and sisters with whom you have lived in the past; they too will show themselves to you. Travel of course is another thing that will change completely. Your spacecraft can then be powered by this photon energy, and therefore there will be so much more benefit in future because the craft will be light and manoeuvrable, and not need rocket fuel and complicated systems. It will be much more straightforward for those who are involved in manufacturing and designing these craft.

Travel will be simple because you can teleport across your own planet through thought. Think of a place that you would wish to be, and you will be there! It will be a completely different lifestyle for you, and you will find that aircraft will become obsolete in time, once people have grown accustomed to travelling in this way. Apart from everything else, the fossil fuels will not be necessary in future, and there will be many changes as a result, however, the photon energy will be simple, and if people wish to have some other kind of transport, it can be fuelled by using this energy that will be in great abundance, and will be utilised by those who have the ability to harness it and use it for the vehicles that will be required.

At present on the Earth there is much darkness, negativity and violence. This occurs in pockets throughout the Earth, and you will find that in time these pockets will gradually dissipate and work their way out of the Earth. The lightworkers like you will successfully manage to oust the darkness so that the light will overcome the evil that exists at present, and in time, all those involved in negativity will be swept aside. Everything is waiting for you, and you will realise that my words are coming true when the time comes. You perhaps have some doubts, and that there will be danger involved, and that there may be loss of life when the photon belt arrives, but do not fear, all those on the spiritual path will be safe and their families protected. It is only those of a violent nature who will be swept off the Earth at this time.

It is difficult to say how this will be done, because your minds are finite, and cannot always accept everything that we can do, but believe me, it will be the separation of the sheep from the goats, shall we say, or the flowers and the weeds, perhaps that is a better analogy. So that those who have strewn the path with flowers, the lightworkers who project goodness and purity in their lives, will be given that protection from us. We have been working towards this end as you know for so long, and we know that you have the faith to continue and walk forth into the new day to be the new humanity that has been prophesied for a long time. So now you progress into the new Heaven and the new Earth that has been waiting for you. It is a time of great excitement; it is a wonderful time to be alive. You have chosen well, and you still have work ahead of you, but that work will gather momentum, and you will achieve much over this next year through our help.

Those who are working between the different levels of being, the different dimensions, and ourselves who have lived this life of Mastership for many centuries, have the capability of protecting you all, working for the good of the whole. The universe itself will welcome you with open arms into this new life that you will be stepping into in a short space of time. I will tell you more in my next talk, but for now God bless and keep you all. Master R.

TEACHINGS FROM THE ASCENDED MASTERS–9

This is Master R, my greetings to you dear ones, and fellow workers in the light. I wish to speak on many things today, and try to expand your thinking further as time progresses. There is so much to accept in this time of change, and I know that you have gradually been regarding the change as something that will occur quite soon. Time is fleeting by, and gradually, imperceptibly you are changing. You have been told that your chakra system is altering, and making you a new type of person. You are becoming able to receive much more telepathic communication in the future.

The chakras on the head are expanding so that you have a type of antenna ready to receive and transmit signals to one another, and to receive these signals from other beings of light. You will be told in the future how to protect yourselves, in order to protect these new antenna, so you don't receive any signals you do not wish to receive. Rather like the protection around your third eye and the crown chakra at present that are particularly vulnerable. Remember always to close down your chakras after meditating, you know this, but even more now, and in the future, this protection is essential. But we will explain further at a future time, just remember to always protect these areas.

As time progresses, your bodies will change and become more ethereal. It is when the photon belt comes closer to Earth that you have to think of these things more. Gradually it is looming large on the horizon, and the Earth is gradually preparing to receive the photon energy when the meeting occurs. As I have told you, the Earth including the rest of the solar system, will be engulfed in the photon belt. This halo of photon energy and light will surround the Earth, but you will be in this protective bubble that is being prepared for you, and all will be well. It is only the darkness and cold that you may feel is very strange for those few days, for which you can prepare yourselves. It is only the edge of the photon belt that creates this dark and cold, because of the shutting out of your sun, moon and stars for the time being, but you can rest assured that once you have gone through that edge of the photon belt, things will change for the better in every way.

The whole atmosphere of the solar system including Earth will be cleansed and purified by the photon energy, the only danger being that nuclear reactors may be compressed by this photon energy, and there may be some danger of radiation from those areas. We are hoping that this will be nullified, and will do all in our power to prevent anything drastic from occurring. You will be protected as you have been told, and once you come out into the sunshine, then you will know that all is well, and that your lives will be altered into a new lifestyle completely. As I mentioned, electrical systems will be useless at that time, and you will accept that the four days of darkness will come to an end and you will come through it quite safely. Your bodies will become light after this compression of the few days, and they will be charged with photon energy. You will be able to see things you have never seen in your lives, all the Devic beings and the Angelic Hierarchy will gradually show themselves to you, and you will discover much that at present of which you are unaware.

Your new chakra systems will be extended at that time, so that you can accept all these telepathic impulses that will be propelled to you, and you will be able to contact one another through the mind in future days. As you gradually become accustomed to this new ability, you will find it will develop and be a very satisfactory means of communication with one another. You have been expanding your minds over time to accept increasingly more new ideas and possibilities. As Sananda told you some time ago, many truths that until now you had only thought rather strange, but now you can see that they are the truth. The fact that at the time of Jesus' birth when the star was seen moving towards Bethlehem, shining down on all who were concerned with the birth of Christ Jesus. You now know that it was a spacecraft shining its light down on the Earth, and that the craft was from the future. At the time when Sananda spoke of this, he did not say that it was from the future because it was enough for you to accept that it was a spacecraft and not a star.

I think that in the Bible story, everyone accepted that it was a star because in the days when you were younger, spacecraft were not spoken of or indeed thought about until more recently, when science fiction stories were launched. Gradually over the last few decades, they have become extremely popular, and as a result people are ready to accept more now than they would have when you were a child. Now you are all ready to accept many things that now reveal themselves to you as the truth, that the burning bush written of in the Bible was in fact a spacecraft, and that many descriptions in the Bible represent spacecraft. In those days how could they know what it was? So gradually you come to realise that spacecraft have existed for millennia. Over the centuries discoveries have been made of many more planets and stars that in the past were not known. Nowadays, as time progresses, more discoveries are being made, and if you open your minds still further, you can recognise the fact that in the past these spacecraft may have come from the future, and not from the present time. At that time in the past, time travel and other dimensions were unheard of, but you know better now, and as you think of these things, new horizons present themselves to you, and perhaps your mind becomes rather mixed up as these new thoughts assemble and reassemble themselves in your mind as you try to make sense of it.

Suffice to say that you are learning and accept increasingly more as the years go by, and you will find that you should just accept in faith what you feel is right. Always question things as they are told you, and as you read them in books, not everything is the pure truth, as you know. You have to sometimes take things with a pinch of salt, as you say, and decide for yourselves what in your heart you feel is the truth. When you are ready to accept it with your heart, then you know that it is so. I am attempting to explain these things to you gradually. I know that you do not want too much detail, because it is difficult enough to accept all these new ideas as it is.

Scientists have been working on new ways of powering all forms of transport that use fossil fuels, and also spacecraft. As you are aware, the spacecraft need massive amounts of fuel to counteract the gravity pull of the Earth, and over the past decade or so, there have been ideas put forward for new forms of energy that have been shelved and rethought about as time has gone by. It has been difficult for them to create some new form of energy strong enough to fuel these craft to be sufficiently safe for them to reach out to the stars. It takes time to create a new fuel, and a new way of projecting these craft into space, or any sort of missile into the air. In time, this photon energy that has been discovered by scientists will be utilised to the full, and when you have merged with the photon belt, it will be there in abundance to be used for craft and various other means of transport in the future.

At present, mankind has to rely on the fossil fuels for heating, transport, and cooking. Everything depends on this, but in the future there will be many changes, as I said, and in fact there will not be the necessity to eat as much as you do at present. As your bodies become more amorphous, you will find that you need less to fuel and propel you, especially when you use teleportation, you will not need any energy apart from your minds, using thought as a means of transport, in time. Many miraculous things will occur once you have reached the photon belt, and even before then. If you can achieve access to the fourth dimension before that, and subsequently the fifth, then you will be able to do these things before the photon belt energy surrounds you.

Times are changing fast for you and for all others who are concerned with these spiritual changes, and physical changes to a certain extent. All of you who are on the spiritual path are ready, and will be able to help others when the time comes for this radical change. You will be able to explain what is occurring and help them through this time. We, the Masters have been attempting to help all who are aware, all who are awakened, and will guide you through this time. There will be others from those planets who have been surrounding the Earth with their craft over the last decade or two, and they will help you before this time comes, you will be counselled and helped. The explanation will be given to you, so that you can protect yourselves for those days of darkness that will come to all in the solar system, but all is well and you will be protected always.

Do keep working with the light, and using it to good effect for the good of all of you, all humanity and the Earth herself. You have been sending light out towards Lyra and her inhabitants who need this help at present, and much has been done to good effect for them, and will continue to help them through their troubled time. We are working with many beings of light from all the planets that have a benevolent attitude to the Earth. Everything is in order, and prepared in readiness for you. Be of good cheer, and know that you are in good hands. All of you have the ability to send forth the light to all who need it, and in time that light will be very effective against those dark negative areas that still inhabit the Earth. Those areas are gradually dispersing, and less violence will occur in the future as this dispersal continues. The saying 'it is always darkest before the dawn' is very true, and the violence that is occurring at present is the prelude to the dawn of your new beginning. God bless and keep you all. Master R.

TEACHINGS OF THE ASCENDED MASTERS-10

My greetings of love to you all, this is Master R. Having established that you have now been extending your chakra system, and gradually building a more powerful antenna to receive telepathic communication now and in the future, you will realise that it is an important factor in your lives, and that, as I have said, protection will be required even more than previously to your chakra system. So, always after meditation it is very important to close down. Beginning at the top above your head, that is the most vulnerable of all. In the future you will be using this communication system to establish a rapport between yourselves and many beings. Once you have started using this, you will find that you can receive communications more easily from the realms of light, and in future days, you will be able to communicate with other beings from planets yet unknown to you. Those who presently channel will be able to extend their areas of communication.

This is all for a purpose in the future, because not only will you be communicating with one another telepathically once you have passed into the photon belt, and perhaps before that, but you will be communicating and receiving from other beings, those from other planets and the Angelic Hierarchy and ourselves, the Masters. You will all have this facility built in, and therefore it is important to understand that you will be part and parcel of a whole federation of the galaxy, you are becoming a part of the whole. Perhaps in the past you have felt strange longings to be a part of everything on occasions. Those of you particularly who are most sensitive have perhaps looked at a beautiful sunset and felt that you were excluded from this. Well, in the future you will be part of it. You can receive from all beings who are benevolent towards you, and you will realise that your consciousness will expand tremendously to enfold the whole of the cosmic consciousness.

It is a very large subject to cover in one talk, because it is a completely new concept for you to realise, that you will be linking with many beings at present who encircle the Earth in their spacecraft. They have been working towards establishing this rapport between humanity and themselves because they have been waiting for humanity to awaken to this new capability that is beginning. You have been told that humanity came from the stars originally, and all of you have come from a star system or another planet in one of your previous early incarnations. Obviously this is something that the general public as a whole are completely unaware of. They know that in the past there has been some form of civilisation that has built the pyramids, and has established various centres throughout the world that have been forgotten over the millennia.

There is the Mayan civilisation and the Incas, and there have been many things that are mysterious, perhaps, to those who are not aware of the fact that beings from worlds who are highly technically evolved, established pyramids and other structures that have, over that great period of time, been overgrown by jungle or disappeared through Earth movement. This is not important because you are aware that all these things that were built so long ago could not possibly have been built by Neolithic, Neanderthal man or Stone Age man, which was believed to have happened in the past. It is utterly ridiculous to imagine that this primitive creature could possibly have conceived any of these brilliant structures. Think of the statues of Easter Island and at Abu Simbel on the Nile. All of these giant carvings and buildings that had been built in past centuries, which have somehow been constructed, and some fabled story made up to cover the missing areas of history. Everything that has been constructed that seems strange, like the Nazca Plain configurations, and which could only be seen from the air were obviously done by beings who were highly skilled.

Everything that has happened can then be realised to be making sense if in the past mankind had come from a highly evolved planet or star. Therefore, once you have accepted this fact, and realised that all of you are originally from the stars, then you will recognise that all these beings in the craft are related to you in some way from past times, and all of them ready to greet you and welcome you into this new hierarchy, of which you will be an important part. You will be accepted with love and greeted wholeheartedly by all these beings who are waiting to accept you into their civilisation.

What will happen in the future is that you will all be capable of doing things that at present are only a dream to you. You have been told that you will be capable of travelling through thought, and you will be capable of creating many things through your minds. It may seem that this will be impossible to you, but hold on to this idea, because it is the truth, and it will occur in time. I know it is difficult to have the faith to accept this, and to recognise the fact that in time you too will be a part of this great consciousness that surrounds you, and which you are only barely aware of. Realise it and be thankful, and ready to look forward to this new life that will unfold in front of you.

There is at present a change in the awareness of many other people who up to now have just been living a normal existence, shall we say, without thinking of future days being different from the present. They too are reading more, and watching more on television, programmes that they would not have considered some years back. Things to expand their awareness that include what you might call science fiction, but as you have been becoming aware, truth is stranger than fiction, and people are becoming more enlightened about space craft, UFOs and the like, over recent times, but even so, they still cannot grasp the fact that Earth herself is changing, and that they too are changing. It is difficult to alter a lifetime of normal experience, and to realise that this will be changed forever once you have reached the fourth and fifth dimensions, and they are rapidly approaching. Some are already moving into this dimension and finding that they have a different attitude to life.

There will be no death as you have known it in the past, and I know that you have been told this, but it is difficult to grasp, that you will continue experiencing, learning and evolving from now on. There will be some who will pass into the transition known as death before this occurs, but in the main, there will be a continuous life cycle, and you will become what they call, fully conscious beings. You will gradually evolve your DNA to what it was originally, and this is most important, that you receive the extra strands that were taken from you long ago in Atlantean times, and then you will be able to reconstruct your DNA to what it should be. It is difficult for you to realise that this is the reason that the capability of telepathy has been lost to you from many centuries ago. It has been latent and rather difficult to expand the consciousness up to now, but as I have said, that capability will return to you, and you will find that you can be capable of this new communication system in the future.

As a result of your new communications with other beings, you will find that the trivial problems that have been troubling mankind over these past centuries will dwindle and become nothing. The differences between race, colour, creed and sex will be non- existent, and you will find that humanity will come together as one, and there will be new legislation that will come from an international government of some kind. It will be led by those who are capable of being in contact with the beings from other worlds and with us, and willing to cooperate. It is important that this will be so. There are certain members of that group of people who are ready to accept their new responsibilities and work with a large transworld government, which will appoint new members to link with other beings. All this will come in the future, and the petty squabbling between small factions will not occur. There will be a linking between the countries of the world and there will be unity that has never been known before, because you as a planet will unite and form a strong bond. This is important that Earth should be peaceful and ready to welcome other beings linking with them. They are benevolent towards you, and all of them are working for the good of the whole, for the whole of the cosmos and your galaxy. So you must expand your thoughts to include this into your new thinking.

At present you may think that this will be completely impossible, for humanity to work together as one, but you must realise that this new change coming into the photon belt when the darkness descends will alter many things and many outlooks of those who in the past have only hoped for power and are greedy for this. Everything of this kind will change, and there will be a new unity that will bring out the best in all of you, rather like when catastrophes occur, such as during world war two, when there was bombing and people lost their homes and families. Even now, when there has been a bomb left, and people have been killed and maimed, it always brings out that unity and love, that is there within each one of you. Realise that this love will expand within each one of you, and that is what will rule the Earth, and the whole solar system linking you together, and those who are here to help you like us, will guide you through this change, and help you in your new attitude towards the future. You will be given counselling and help by those who are aware of what is about to occur.

Accept these words that are the truth, and I know that you look forward to this new life. Everything will continue, but it will be a completely trouble free life, where wars are non-existent, violence is non-existent, and the children who are emerging through this will have a future that you might have envied in the past. It is something that they can look forward to, for their education will continue, and they will evolve into beings of great capability and love. All is well. God bless and keep you. Master R.

TEACHINGS FROM THE ASCENDED MASTERS-11

My greetings to you all, this is Master R. I think that all of you have been aware of changes around you. There are new energies that are pouring down on mankind and recharging him, so there is a sense of accomplishment gradually forming within you. You have been concentrating on regular meditation and gradually there is a build up of confidence, and the knowledge that you exist on many levels when you are meditating. Mankind is awakening to the fact that he is one with all beings. Many things have occurred since the Harmonic Convergence in August 1987 when pure energy was poured down onto you, and those others who were already on the spiritual path. You are all members of the 144,000 who were scattered throughout the Earth; that number which was mentioned in the Bible. You have all received these energies and are rising gradually to that higher vibration, and you are realising on reflection that there has been much achieved over these last few years.

Think of the communications that have been received in various ways. The channelling that have been accomplished by so many over these past years, and new channels already appearing daily, who will take over and be able to achieve much more than those who have been doing this work in the past. It matters not the level of the channelling, it is the intent, and the fact that so many have been attempting to bring our wisdom to all. There are many other ways in which information has been received from the stars, shall we say, and from us the Hierarchy. Think of the crop circles that have been appearing over the years, and have become much more complex. It is something that has appealed to a broad spectrum of the population. Some of you may not have perceived what the crop circles are attempting to tell you, but it is important that others who are perhaps not on the spiritual path, but aware of their capabilities in scientific and mathematical terms, it is they who have arrived at some solutions. The diagrams made by these circles represent more to them than perhaps those of you who are working with us already, and as a result, they are being brought into the puzzle, into the mystery that is what you are living at present.

Life is always a mystery in many ways. You travel along life's highway wondering what is around the corner for you and your loved ones, and in future times the mystery deepens because man is heir to so much more than he is at present. It is a time of wonder and excitement for the future, because man is rising onto a higher dimension than ever before in known years of history. Perhaps in the first early days when man appeared on the planet from the stars, shall we say, those days are lost in antiquity, but you are realising now increasingly more, that humanity had not always inhabited this planet. As has been said before, there was an indigenous race that existed, but we have talked about species who had arrived in spacecraft, and were considered to be gods because of their knowledge and miraculous powers to those who originally lived in the areas where they appeared. Nonetheless, mankind had developed in fits and starts, shall we say, throughout the globe, and has achieved much in many ways, both physically, materially and spiritually, and over the millennia humanity has changed remarkably. Unfortunately at present, there is that large factor of violence and negativity that has to be diminished before the time of the change.

As the photon belt nears, the Earth changes will occur faster. You will realise that time is already speeding up, and we progress, the time will accelerate even faster, and therefore you must be ready to accept the fact that alterations will be made in that time. You realise that in the past, alterations were made to mankind, and perhaps you felt a sense of outrage to hear that the DNA had been reduced in the past. Experiments had been made in Atlantean times by many members from other planets, but this is all past history, and now you are building up your DNA so that you will be capable of what man was able to do when he first achieved miraculous occurrences on this planet. It has been said before that you have come from many planets, and originated there, bringing with you that knowledge that you gained over past incarnations. It may be that you have incarnated many times on Earth, who knows, but this matters not. It is this incarnation that is the most important for you all, because you are taking part in a great ascension. You are becoming one with all of us, and gradually, slowly but surely, you are realising what has been occurring over these past years is culminating in this great happening, which is all part of God's Plan. We the Masters have been participating in this, as you know, and helping to pour down energies to guide you through this.

I know that you have been considering many things over these past few months, and realise that everything that has happened in the past is a basis for your lives. Perhaps I am not putting this succinctly enough, but consider how you have always clung to the fact that your religion was based upon the life of Jesus and his disciples, and the teachings given by them in the Bible. Everything was based on this, and you have been questioning this and have always done so over the years, for those of you who are of this faith are making sure that your belief system was correct, and that you believed in the one true God, Father of all. All religions are based on a God, a powerful Creator, and this is so, but you have recently heard that the Bible story was slightly different, and that the star that shone over Bethlehem was a spacecraft, and this was rather disconcerting to you. I know that obviously this is not going to change the fact that Jesus was born at this time, it is just that the linking of the two together seems strange to you, after being aware of the story in the Bible throughout your lives, talking of a star and spacecraft were not mentioned obviously. Now you may realise that many other stories, legends and myths that you read as a child are based on true facts, and that the giants that were mentioned in many legends have existed upon the Earth in the past, having come from different planets. Other stories that mention gods descending from a chariot of fire, obviously speak of spacecraft, and beings from other worlds descending. Many things have been made clear to you, and your minds have become accustomed to the strange stories that are the truth rather than fiction. Your minds have become much more open than they were, and perhaps you have helped others to have open minds to new ideas.

There are more things that will occur over the next year or so, and you know that you will be given counselling and help over that time before the change occurs. If you look back over the last ten years you will, on reflection, discover many factors that have slotted into place. It is rather like a large jigsaw covering the Earth, and all the pieces are gradually fitting together and making sense. We on our part can see this occurring. It is much easier for us from our point of view to get the overall picture of your lives taking shape over these years, and in time you will realise that everything that has happened is for the good, and that in time you who are on the spiritual path will find life becoming easier. It is always difficult to be different from the mass, and to try to live truly the way that your heart wishes you to do. You must be true to yourselves and to your work in service to God and spirituality.

Everything that is occurring now is part of God's Plan, and I know that you are attempting to stand up and be counted, and to attempt to explain things to those who are not yet fully awakened. It is time for all to awaken to this new age, this spiritual age of the mind. Mind power is essential and is of the future, it is time now for you to realise that thought is becoming increasingly more important, and must be used positively and for good. This mind power is what will be used to communicate with in future days, more than the voice, and is something that is important to explain to others, to keep their thoughts positive and pure, and not to add to the negativity that is already abounding on the Earth, but which will be overcome, never fear. Good will always prevail, the light against the darkness. You are becoming more confident in your way of life, and will spread the word we feel sure, so that more will join you in daily meditation and upliftment in future days. All is going well in God's Plan, and you are fulfilling your part in that Plan, so for now I leave you with my blessing, and the knowledge that we are always here whenever you wish for help.
God bless. Master R.

MASTER R's INVOCATION

As was given in book one, we shall conclude with this simple Invocation to the Light, which is powerful, that asks for Michael the archangel to be present.

"Wielder of the Sword of Light come forth.
Defend man from his darkness.
May God's pure Divine Light shine through the hearts of men,
And love and peace prevail."

FOR THOSE NEW TO CHANNELLING

For anyone who has not so far heard of channelling I shall explain about it here.

Channelling normally occurs after the recipient has become accustomed to meditating regularly, and is a form of message taking from higher realms.

During meditation, he or she is used to listening to that still small voice within, not really a voice, but thoughts that are dropped into the mind by their guide or, eventually, a higher being such as an angel or master.

There is normally a signal given, such as a slight pressure on the top of the head, which is what I experienced, as a sign to take notice, and to still any random thoughts and listen within.

The Ascended Masters are souls who have incarnated many times and overcome every difficulty experienced by mankind, and triumphed over all adversities that man is heir to.

They have become true Masters of everything, and only wish to help mankind in whatever way they can.

They are members of the White Brotherhood, who exist mainly in spirit form, and who gather in a remote area of the Himalayas, and other remote places around the world.

BERYL CHARNLEY - PUBLICATIONS

1. Channelled Communications from the Devic Kingdom.

2. Channelled Communications from Sirius, Arcturus, Pleiades and Betelgeuse.

www.ingramcontent.com/pod-product-compliance
Lightning Source LLC
Chambersburg PA
CBHW061643040426
42446CB00010B/1547